The Mind of the Sailor

Huge seas in the Southern Ocean. Waves like this test boat and crew, but more voyages are ruined by quarrels and incompatibility than by heavy weather. PHOTO: *Jimmy Cornell*

The Mind of the Sailor

An exploration of the human stories behind adventures and misadventures at sea

Peter Noble and Ros Hogbin

ADLARD COLES NAUTICAL
London

Published 2001 by Adlard Coles Nautical
an imprint of A & C Black (Publishers) Ltd
37 Soho Square, London W1
www.adlardcoles.co.uk

ISBN 0-7136-5025-7

A CIP catalogue record for this book is available from the British Library.

Note: While all reasonable care has been taken in the publication of this book, the
publisher takes no responsibility for the use of the methods or products described in
the book.

Photographs are by the authors unless otherwise stated.

Printed and bound in the USA.

Contents

Acknowledgements

The idea for this book developed from my own sailing experiences and from conversations on boats in anchorages and harbours on both sides of the Atlantic. As I listened to sailors talk about the sea and the fellowship of sailing, I realised how much there is to learn about the psychology of sailing, and how the mind of the sailor can be as fascinating as the sea.

Some of the ideas expressed here have a basis in my earlier articles and seminars. It was Jimmy Cornell, formerly of the organisation World Cruising, who first suggested that they should be developed into a book and I am grateful to him for his enthusiastic help at every stage. Jimmy also allowed me to include some of his wonderful photographs, and World Cruising made facilities available to interview crews in the Atlantic Rally for Cruisers (ARC) and in round the world races.

In preparation, I have listened to many sailors and read books and scientific articles. The chapter references give only a few key sources among hundreds. In particular, I am grateful to Oliver Wall for allowing me to include his contribution to the *Apollonia* tragedy.

My wife Joan has been a constant source of help and encouragement. Ros and I also wish to thank Janet Murphy and Sarah Stirling, our editors at Adlard Coles Nautical, for their endless patience and encouragement.

Peter Noble

Of all the questions an interviewer can ask, the 'why' question can sometimes be the hardest to answer, especially for a book of this nature. I am therefore most grateful to the sailors who sat with me, took time to talk about their lives, and answered my many 'whys'.

Sir Chay Blyth had me, in turns, both riveted and roaring with laughter as he described his early life, sporting exploits and sailing challenges. Both Sir Chay (Executive Chairman) and Simon Walker (Managing Director) impressed me with their descriptions of the Challenge Business and how it has developed over recent years. I was fortunate enough to catch the two female skippers for BT Global Challenge 2000, Lin Parker and Alex Phillips, while at St Katharine's Dock, and welcomed their viewpoints.

Tony Bullimore took time out of a very busy fund-raising and boat preparation schedule to see me. Diana Garside shared her experiences with me, both as crew volunteer in the 1996 BT Global Challenge and as shore team for Mike Garside's 1998 Around Alone campaign. Mike Garside, whom I would term 'the thinking man's adventurer', gave me much food for thought with his insights into singlehanded sailing. Mike Golding fascinated me with his competitive focus and commitment to Grand Prix racing, and Pete Goss somehow managed to find time for a quick 'phone interview' with me in the run-up to the launch of his catamaran *Team Philips*. Sir Robin Knox-Johnston's absorbing recollections gave me a valuable guided tour through modern sailing history, from his own pioneering circumnavigation to the Jules Verne challenge and his Clipper Ventures. Finally, of the many people I met, Ellen MacArthur inspired me enormously with her life story (so far!) and her infectious enthusiasm for sailing in general and world-class racing in particular. Many thanks also to Mark Turner of Offshore Challenges, who fitted me in to see Ellen before her last-minute dash out of the London Boat Show and on to a New Zealand-bound plane.

A number of sailors committed their ideas to paper. Thank you to Naomi James, for taking the trouble to consider my written requests and responding so thoughtfully. Anne Hammick replied to my questions, as well as making suggestions about additional cruising skippers to contact. Anna Brunyee and Fran Flutter also spent time at their desks, and Lady Denise Evans responded enthusiastically to my phone call.

Thank you to the staff at the National Maritime Museum's Caird Library and to Michael Howe, the Librarian at the Cruising Association, who was a great help in locating scores of books and making additional suggestions along the way.

Most of all, thanks to Andrew Hogbin, my best friend in sailing and in life.

Ros Hogbin

Foreword

by Sir Chay Blyth

The Mind of the Sailor is a timely reminder to amateurs and professionals alike that safe and successful sailing depends ultimately on the individuals involved and their frame of mind. No amount of high tech electronics or fancy foul weather gear or the latest sail technology will by themselves see sailors safely home, but determination to face-down dangers and disappointment and to see a plan fully realised and completed will.

The world is full of talented people who seem to promise a great deal, but labour at the margins of life and never fully deliver. On the other hand, there are those who are apparently less talented and of whom less is expected, but who

Sir Chay Blyth PHOTO: *Adrian Rayson*

take the world by storm and exceed what early promise they may have shown in huge and startling measure. The gulf between these two types lies in their determination to achieve. Whatever goals someone may set themselves, or have set for them, the chances of success, of reaching that goal, are determined first and last in the mind.

Sailing today is a sophisticated business. All kinds of labour-saving devices can now be found on board even quite small craft: electric winches, self-deploying spinnakers and self-furling sails have gone a long way to take some of the sheer physical slog out of working a boat, and with satellite navigation the success or failure of a voyage is more and more down to the sailors themselves and to their strength of mind. How they react to adverse weather, equipment failure or in the case of bigger boats, an argumentative crew, will very often determine the outcome of a voyage.

Sailing provides examples of the indomitable nature of the human spirit and anyone who takes to the sea in a boat will recognise the challenge. Travellers on the ocean, whether running before a storm or dipping quietly through the night beneath a warm and seamless quilt of stars, will come to thank Peter Noble and Ros Hogbin for exploring, in this challenging and intriguing book, the importance of strength of will, mental attitude and determination.

Sir Chay Blyth
Executive Chairman
Challenge Business

The Authors

Peter Noble is a consultant psychiatrist and for many years was on the staff of the Maudsley Hospital and the Institute of Psychiatry, London. He is also an experienced yachtsman who has cruised extensively, and made Atlantic crossings in his 34-foot sloop *Artemis*. He is the author of many scientific articles and books. In recent years his interest in the mind and the sea has been united in a series of articles on the psychology of sailing.

Ros Hogbin is a writer and journalist, who has recently returned from a three-year circumnavigation with her husband on their Nicholson 43. She has sailed since childhood and taken part in the Fastnet Race and the Phuket King's Cup Regatta. She has written on cruising and racing for *Sailing Today* and *Yachting World* and is currently editing *The Pacific Crossing Guide* (second edition) as well as working on a book of her sailing travels.

Introduction

Anyone who goes to sea in a small sailing boat will feel far more than the physical sensation of wind in the sails and movement across the water. The challenges and joys experienced when facing the elements and harnessing their natural power have tested seafarers for centuries, and are quite unlike those met on land. There is something about travelling across the open sea that has a profound psychological effect on the sailor.

This book considers the emotional and intellectual aspects of sailing and how they affect cruising and racing yachtsmen alike. It covers a broad range of topics which will appeal to anyone fascinated by the sea and its effects on the sailor. Each chapter focuses on a different type of sailing experience: specific historical events and misadventures at sea, tips for living the cruising lifestyle harmoniously, and interviews with present-day sailing personalities.

The Mind of the Sailor begins by looking at the mixture of qualities found in the successful skipper, as well as the importance of promoting harmony on board. The particular stresses and strains of the long distance cruising lifestyle and the difficulties of breaking free from shore life are also featured.

Chapters covering events from the past consider Captain Bligh and ask why he precipitated mutiny not only in the *Bounty*, but also in several other ships under his command. The intense psychological pressure surrounding Donald Crowhurst when he disappeared at sea in 1969 is examined, as well as the events leading up to murder on the cruising yacht *Apollonia* in 1981. A number of racing yachtsmen in the 1979 Fastnet Race chose to abandon ship. What drove them to this course of action and how did it affect their likelihood of survival?

Sailing personalities, including Sir Chay Blyth, Sir Robin Knox-Johnston, Ellen MacArthur and Naomi James, give their views on the sport with answers to questions about why sailors race alone across the world's most inhospitable oceans and how the communications revolution has affected the way we sail. Other chapters describe the rise of women skippers and the modern development of extreme sailing. The final chapter concentrates on the many positive aspects of the sport and gives an insight into why, in the face of struggle, physical discomfort and danger, there is still a very real 'joy of sailing'.

Peter Noble and Ros Hogbin

What Makes a Good Skipper?
What Makes a Good Crew?

• Peter Noble •

This first question – 'What makes a good skipper?' – is one that is often asked. Most skippers believe that they are 'good' – the crew sometimes disagree. In most countries there are no minimum requirements to be a skipper – beyond the ability to buy, borrow or hire a boat. Even the prestigious Yachtmaster examinations mainly test technical skills and are less concerned with leadership or with the ability to run a 'happy' ship or an 'efficient' ship. In fact, the two – technical skills and leadership skills – are often the same. It is the quality of the skipper that determines both the safety and the pleasure of the voyage. Like everything else in life, skippers vary enormously. Almost everyone who has crewed for several skippers has at some time or other left a boat vowing never to sail on her again!

Psychological studies

Obviously a good skipper must have adequate sailing experience and skills, but these technical skills alone do not make a good leader. There is no single rigid stereotype of the 'good' skipper; much depends on circumstances. A style of leadership appropriate to the Tsarist navy is not best suited to a holiday along a sheltered coast.

A yacht at sea is a small isolated community and has much in common with other isolated communities where leadership is of paramount importance. Such groups include mountaineering and polar expeditions, air crew, and military and naval units, and scientific studies have produced a lot of information about the working relationships in these groups. It has become clear that the personality and attitude of the leader are both very important to the efficiency of the group. With regard to this, air crew and astronauts have been studied intensively, and I have applied the results of these studies to yachtsmen taking part in round the world rallies and races. The results of studies on air crew are particularly relevant to yachting.

Successful pilots show a characteristic personality profile. They tend to be active and achievement orientated, with strong needs for mastery and control. In a crisis they respond in active and practical ways. An active response to danger tends to reduce anxiety, while passivity may lead to a sense of helplessness and panic. Many pilots are amateur yachtsmen in their spare time and they usually make excellent skippers.

Successful leaders score highly for a trait that psychologists dub 'expressivity'. In this context 'expressivity' involves personal warmth, sensitivity to the feelings of others, and an ability to discuss as well as to command. These are the qualities that are important in leading and managing people, and this is an area in which the skills of the amateur skipper often need improvement.

What makes a bad leader? Again, military and aviation studies show that certain personal qualities are particularly associated with poor leadership and lead to poor morale and poor achievement by the team. These qualities include emotional coldness, verbal aggression, rigidity, and a tendency to be over-critical and indifferent to the feelings of others. These harmful traits have been dubbed 'negativity'.

Three famous leaders: Bligh, Shackleton and Scott

The achievements of three famous historical figures – Captain Bligh, captain of the *Bounty*; Sir Ernest Shackleton, the explorer and sailor; and Captain Robert Falcon Scott, the Antarctic explorer – illustrate how the personality of the leader influences outcome and may be crucial to success or failure.

The story of Captain Bligh is told in Chapter 4. Bligh was intelligent, capable and honourable, but he was also rigid, overbearing and over-critical – a prime example of negativity. From time to time a 'Captain Bligh syndrome' can be observed in the skippers of small yachts. This is when a normally reasonable and courteous individual, usually a middle-aged man, assumes command of a pleasure boat only to become domineering, over-critical and sometimes foul-mouthed. This most often happens when a boat is chartered, for a person who charters a vessel is likely to be less experienced than an owner and unlikely to know the boat well. This lack of experience and competence leads to insecurity, making it difficult to manage the boat in a relaxed way. Pride may prevent the skipper from admitting to difficulties or asking for help. The apparent 'change of character' is, in reality, a reaction to stress and anxiety. On a more minor level, I am also sure that stress and anxiety contribute to the irritability that is often displayed by skippers.

The explorer Shackleton was an excellent sailor and comes close to the stereotype of the ideal leader. His standards were high, but he preferred a style of approval and encouragement rather than criticism. He was sensitive to the feelings of others and to the emotional relationships within the group. In 1916 he was forced to abandon his ship, *Endurance*, which was crushed by the Antarctic ice pack. He left the main party behind and gained help by sailing one of the ship's boats some 800 miles across the Roaring Forties and the stormy South Antarctic Ocean to the nearest settlement in South Georgia. This was an incredible 16-day voyage in a 21-foot open boat with a small crew. When one crew member lost his gloves, Shackleton offered him his own, and even threatened to throw the gloves overboard when the man initially refused to take them. Shackleton was also able to delegate – for instance, he wrote of the deputy left in charge of the shore party: 'I practically left the whole situation and scope of action and decision to his own judgement secure in the knowledge he would act wisely.' In spite of immense privations and difficulties, Shackleton did not lose a single life on this expedition. He was revered by his men, many of whom accompanied him on several later expeditions.

Robert Falcon Scott conforms to that favourite English stereotype, the gallant failure. He led two expeditions to the Antarctic and, with four companions, reached the South Pole on 17 January 1912. But the Norwegian explorer Amundsen had preceded him. Blizzards and illness delayed Scott's return journey and the entire party perished within a few miles of safety. The tragic story of the journey is known in detail from the diaries of Scott and his companions, although after his death Scott became a national hero. Scott's temperament was very different from that of Shackleton. Scott was isolated and unconcerned with human feelings, and his immense strength and stamina led him to drive others to the limits of exhaustion. He rarely discussed his plans and had difficulty in delegating. For instance, he left his own base camp with detailed and rigid orders, and it was the very rigidity of these orders that delayed the final rescue effort and contributed to the death of Scott and his party. A strong and dominating temperament of this type may lead to outstanding achievement in difficult circumstances, but too often the authoritarian style of leadership prevents the team from developing its full potential. Scott would have been more suited to being a singlehanded sailor than a yacht skipper.

So what makes a good skipper?

On many occasions I have listened to yacht crews discussing what they believed to be the qualities of a 'good' skipper. The words used were: competent, calm, decisive, friendly, 'able to discuss' and 'able to delegate'. Most experienced skippers are confident and decisive, and are usually able to appear calm even if they do not always feel it. However, the ability to discuss, delegate and remain friendly in the confines of a small boat is more rare. It is deficiencies in this area of leadership, though, that are most likely to cause poor crew morale, a build-up of tensions, and poor teamwork.

Creating a 'happy ship' is not just an inborn knack – thought and effort can contribute to success. This means that the skipper needs to devote as much time, skill and thought to 'running' the crew as to 'running' the boat.

When tensions develop among the crew the skipper should be able to intervene tactfully before these reach crisis point. Try to anticipate difficult situations and talk through a problem before a confrontation occurs. Remember that encouragement is more effective than criticism. A decisive leader should always retain the ability to delegate. A team works best when the individual members can develop a sense of autonomy and achievement. An ability to discuss issues and consider the views of the crew indicates strength not weakness – for we can all learn from the experience of others. When crew are fortunate enough to be sailing with a 'good' skipper, it is instructive for them to think carefully about that particular skipper's style of leadership and management decisions as well as the sailing decisions.

If a personal clash occurs between the skipper and his or her crew, the intelligent skipper does not simply blame the crew, but also questions how different leadership might have helped or avoided the situation.

A round the world race with amateur crew is an extreme test of the qualities of a skipper, and the 1992 British Steel Challenge identified a number of deficiencies in leadership skills. These showed up in tensions and, on occasions, in near mutiny; on one yacht the skipper had to be replaced. The race organiser, Sir Chay Blyth, applied the lessons learnt from the 1992 race to the 1996 BT Global Challenge. More care was taken in crew selection, and the induction training of the skippers was increased to three weeks.

Management trainees and consultants have recognised the potential of these races for the development of leadership and performance skills. MaST International, a management training organisation that describes itself as 'a centre for high performance development', analysed the performance of the participants of the 1996 BT Global Challenge. The racing skippers were more likely to be deficient in personal and managerial skills than in technical skills and leadership. MaST International wrote a book, *Global Challenge: Leadership Lessons from 'The World's Toughest Yacht Race'* on the leadership lessons of the race and commented:

> The skippers lacked management skills. They had undertaken a leadership course [three weeks] but not enough time had been devoted to the management element. The fundamental weakness of the majority of skippers lay in their inability to develop the full potential of their teams. They were uncomfortable drawing on the skills of others when they felt that they should know everything themselves. They were extremely good yachtsmen and competent in managing the yacht, but the race is more about the management of *people*.

The author takes a mid-Atlantic sextant reading. Boats have become increasingly technical, but a good skipper does not let himself be too dependent on electronics. PHOTO: *Peter Noble.*

What makes a good crew?

The skipper has a clear job description: he, or she, is in charge of the boat. The role of crew, though, is variable and greatly depends on the particular circumstances. A crew member may be a paying guest on a charter yacht with expectations of being waited on, a complete novice, or someone whose experience and skills are essential to sailing the boat. These varying roles are often complicated by personal and family relationships. On small boats with a crew of two, the couple are often a husband and wife team or sexual partners. In these circumstances the long-term relationship of the couple will bring strengths and sometimes complications to their sailing partnership and interaction as skipper and crew.

In an earlier survey of yacht crews in one round the world rally, skippers were asked to describe their ideal crew. One skipper replied: 'My Aries self steering gear. It doesn't eat, sleep or have an opinion.' I have a lot of sympathy with this view, having sailed over 30,000 miles with my own Aries, and never a cross word, or even a cross thought, between us.

Two qualities are essential for a good crew: motivation and compatibility.

The person must want to make the voyage and be capable of getting along with the skipper and the others on the boat. Taking on board someone who is less than willing, or potentially difficult, is asking for trouble. If there are any doubts, leave the person behind and sail shorthanded, or even single-handed.

The sailing experience of a crew member is helpful, but not all-important. I have made several successful and happy passages with people who had no previous experience whatsoever. An important factor here is motivation – the new crew member must want to learn to sail and to be part of the team. Praise and encouragement from the skipper will foster such motivation. On the other hand, both criticism and unwarranted interference are discouraging and destructive. If the skipper is prepared to teach and to be supportive, even a complete novice can be useful from almost the first moment that he or she sets foot on a boat. Even in this situation, it is important to delegate. I always make novice crew part of the watch rota and let them know that when on watch they are in charge of the boat. I keep a prudent eye on progress, of course, but in a tactful way. It is best not to intervene too soon or too frequently.

Sailing should be enjoyable. People learn best if they have the freedom to make small mistakes and correct them in their own way. An inexperienced skipper may be helped by sailing with more experienced and knowledgeable friends. However, too much reliance on the superior experience of the crew during an ocean voyage can create a dangerous potential for split leadership. In circumstances where the owner lacks experience or confidence, it may be better either to appoint a professional skipper, or to make a less demanding voyage. One must keep in mind, though, that the relationship between a sailing owner and his professional skipper can also be a source of conflict. The situation usually works best when the owner leaves all sailing decisions to the professional skipper. Well-defined leadership is as important for the crew as it is for the skipper.

There is no rigid personality stereotype for a good crew member. Compatibility, which depends on the mix of temperaments, is obviously important. The Europa survey (see Chapter 2) showed that crew members who walked off – or were put off – one boat, often got on well as members of a different crew. Unfortunately, some people are unpopular on any boat while others seem welcome almost anywhere. Good crew members are self-contained and non-intrusive – chattering jollity can become unbearable after even a week at sea. Simple practical matters are very important too. Doing one's fair share of the domestic grind, contributing willingly to jobs at hand, taking turns with the washing-up, and meticulously stowing personal gear so that it does not irritate others are all essential attributes of the good crew member.

Essentially, the main role of each person is to contribute to the working life of the boat and to help ensure a safe passage. The tasks expected will vary

Friendly discussion is often the best way to resolve differences. Skipper and crew talk over tactics before an ocean crossing. PHOTO: *Jimmy Cornell.*

depending on the boat, but a person who is sensitive to the atmosphere on the boat, good humoured and receptive is well on the way to being a good crew member. Crew work under the direction of the skipper, and a good crew is one who listens carefully and is willing and able to take instruction. He or she must also be happy to comply with the routine of the boat. Getting sufficient sleep when off watch, arriving for watches on time, and contributing responsibly to the tasks on board are all part of the job. It also helps not to be over-sensitive – a crew needs to be open to constructive criticism without taking it too personally. Life on a small boat, particularly in heavy weather, can become overcrowded and claustrophobic. Fortunately, some people have the happy knack of diffusing tension and the capacity for overlooking the occasional outburst from other crew, or even from the skipper.

Temperament and compatibility are as important as sailing skills in the choice of a crew. In many ways an ocean passage, with its absence of shipping, shoals and tides, is easier than a coastal cruise. The weather is usually better, and sunshine, blue seas and a fair wind all do wonders for morale. But the situation on a racing yacht is different, where technical competence and physical fitness are much more important. Racing boats also require a larger crew, so the aspiring ocean racer must be prepared for overcrowding and discomfort – this is one of many reasons why I prefer cruising. Crewing a yacht on an ocean crossing, except when racing, does not demand much prior knowledge. A well-motivated and sensible crew member can easily be taught, and learn, on the job. What is essential is the ability to learn to adjust to a lack of autonomy: sleep patterns, mealtimes, diet and alcohol consumption cease to be matters of personal choice, but must, of necessity, be subordinated to the rules of the boat and skipper.

Will I make a good skipper?

Successful and popular skippers, irrespective of whether they are weekend or ocean sailors, have similar personality profiles. They tend to be robust, positive and emotionally warm. They score high on 'expressivity' and low on 'negativity'. I have constructed a questionnaire based on the personality traits and attitudes that are most associated with the capacity to be a good skipper. It has been tested on holiday sailors as well as on skippers and crews in round the world races. Skippers who are highly rated by their crews tend to get good scores on the questionnaire. Experienced crew score only slightly lower than skippers. Obviously it takes much more sailing experience and knowledge to become a good skipper than a good crew, but the personality profiles have much in common. So even if your main role is as crew you may still find it interesting to complete the questionnaire; try to answer the questions honestly and do not cheat. Skippers and crews will find it interesting to compare each other's responses. You may find that other people see you differently from the way you see yourself. The test is intended to be fun, but it is also an opportunity for discussion and improvement.

SKIPPER/CREW QUESTIONNAIRE

Ring Yes or No as appropriate

1 Is getting away from 'difficulties ashore' an important reason for going sailing?

Yes   No

2 Would you find it difficult to give up drinking for a week?

Yes   No

3 Do you become anxious or panicky in confined spaces such as lifts or crowded public transport?

Yes   No

4 When working under pressure do you develop any of the following: headaches, panic attacks, depression, insomnia, anxiety?

Yes   No

5 Do you work best under pressure?

Yes   No

6 Do you find a challenge where others fear a problem?

Yes   No

7 Would most people be better off if they thought less and did more?

Yes   No

8 Do you believe: 'Where there is a will there is a way'?

Yes   No

9 If you receive bad service in a hotel or restaurant, can you complain courteously and without losing your temper?

Yes   No

10 If you play games with friends, is winning more important to you than trying to ensure that the others enjoy themselves?

Yes   No

11 If a friend comes to stay, do you find sharing the use of the bathroom and kitchen difficult?

Yes   No

12 Looking back on parties and social occasions, do you sometimes find that you have said things that you bitterly regret?

Yes   No

13 Have you ever gone on holiday with friends, or another couple, that you thought you knew well, only to find that the holiday ended the friendship?

Yes   No

14 When you drive, are you often in a state of tension or anger because of the behaviour of other drivers?

Yes   No

15 Would you support a crew member who spoke out against a skipper's poor decision with which they disagreed?

Yes   No

16 Do you like to discuss important decisions before making up your mind?

Yes   No

17 If a junior colleague were promoted over you, would you find it difficult to maintain a friendly and effective working relationship?

Yes   No

18 If somebody you know suffers misfortune or bereavement, does shyness or embarrassment prevent you from offering sympathy and help?

Yes   No

19 Can you delegate easily?

Yes   No

20 Is good preparation usually the secret of success?

Yes   No

Scoring

Use the following information to calculate your score:
Questions: 1, 2, 3, 4, 10, 11, 12, 13, 14, 17 and 18: score 1 for every **No**.
Questions: 5, 6, 7, 8, 9, 15, 16, 19 and 20: score 1 for every **Yes**.

Results

15–20	Excellent
10–14	Good
9 and below	Cause for concern

Conclusions from the results

So do you have the personality to become a good skipper? Don't worry if you did not score 20 out of 20 – perfection is rare. Such a high score would probably mean that you had cheated! If you have scored 15 or over, well done. You have the sort of warmth and compatibility that makes it easy for you to lead and to get on with others. A score of between 10 and 14 is average. Pay particular attention to areas highlighted by the questions where you failed to score well. A score of below 9 indicates cause for concern, but it doesn't necessarily mean that you must take up singlehanded sailing. However, if you are going to improve as a skipper you must pay much more attention to your own emotions and how you relate to others. Concentrate on your leadership skills and try to be more sensitive to the attitudes and expectations of your crew.

When tensions develop among the crew, the good skipper should intervene tactfully. If you, as skipper, are upset or angry, try to express your feelings in a reasonable manner. It is always best to deal promptly with emotional problems, including your own, before they reach crisis point. Good communication is essential, and an informal chat at 'happy hour' is a good way of defusing tension. Remember, praise is a more effective way to change behaviour than criticism – remember what happened to Captain Bligh! Avoid 'negativity'. Do not become domineering or over-critical. Be slow to blame others, and when things are done well be sure to say 'thank you'. If a problem occurs, for instance, halyards are tangled or a sail incorrectly hoisted, concentrate on helping the crew to put the problem right, rather than looking for a culprit to blame.

Practical matters are also important. A well-organised watch system maintains morale and harmony as well as safety. The on-watch crew should be temporarily in charge of the boat and know clearly what decisions they are allowed to take. The off-watch crew should be able to relax and recuperate, so that they are alert when they return to duty or have to deal with an emergency. It is important to plan ahead, and most of the work and preparation essential for a happy and successful voyage should have been completed before the boat leaves port.

To recap:

- A good skipper does not become exhausted and irritable by trying to do everything himself or herself.
- A decisive leader retains the ability to delegate.
- A willingness to discuss issues and consider the views of the crew is a sign of strength, not weakness.
- When sailing with a good skipper it can be helpful to think carefully about

the style of leadership and the management decisions as well as the boat handling.

- If a personality clash does occur, the intelligent skipper does not simply blame the crew, but also questions how different leadership might have helped or avoided the situation.
- A good skipper is sensitive to the needs and suggestions of the crew and is, above all, willing to learn. We can all learn from the experience of others.

REFERENCES

Alexander, Caroline, *The Endurance: Shackleton's Legendary Antarctic Expedition*, Bloomsbury Publishing, London, 1998 and Knopf, New York, 1998.

Harrison, A A, Clearwater, Y A, McKay, C P, *From Antarctica to Outer Space: Life in Isolation and Confinement*, Springer-Verlag, New York, 1991.

Nicholas, J M, Penwell, L W, 'A profile of the effective leader in human space flight', *Aviation, Space and Environmental Medicine*, 1995, pp 63–72.

Palkinas, L A, 'Going to extremes: the cultural context of stress, illness and coping in Antarctica', *Society, Science and Medicine*, 1992, pp 651–64.

Picano, J J, 'Personality types among experienced military pilots', *Aviation, Space and Environmental Medicine*, 1991, pp 517–20.

Walters, Humphrey, et al, *Global Challenge: Leadership Lessons from 'The World's Toughest Yacht Race'*, The Book Guild, Sussex, 1997.

Cast Off and Sail Away

• Peter Noble •

In writing this chapter I have been greatly helped by my involvement in the preparations and seminars for the ARC transatlantic rally. Over 150 yachts and 600 crew gather in Gran Canaria and follow the traditional trade wind route to the Caribbean, which was first discovered by Christopher Columbus. The departure in November gives the best chance of a sunny downwind passage, a landfall in time for Christmas and the best of the Caribbean sailing season. It was in the sunshine and bustle of Las Palmas harbour, Gran Canaria, that I listened to the problems and hopes of skippers and crews as they prepared for what, for some, was to be their first ocean crossing.

With the help of my wife, a medical research worker, I also carried out a survey on the skippers and crews who had sailed in the Europa round the world cruising rally. Twenty-nine yachts started from Gibraltar on the first leg of a 24,000-mile competitive circumnavigation, passing through the Panama and Suez canals. This is a trade wind circumnavigation and, not surprisingly, several boats stopped to spend longer in the wonderful warm-weather cruising areas of the Pacific islands. We met the rally in Majorca towards the end of their circumnavigation. At this point, there were still 19 yachts in the race and they had completed 19 of the 20 legs. We asked the skippers and crew to complete a psychological and medical questionnaire, and we also interviewed random participants until the number in our sample had reached 50.

The boats were all moored together by the elegant and spacious Real Club Nautico of Majorca. There was a party atmosphere, and talking to the participants was a delight. The frankest comments were often made in the bar late at night or when sitting enjoying midnight drinks in the cockpit and looking across to the floodlit battlements and medieval buildings of the old harbour and city.

The boats ranged in length from 41 feet to 66 feet. The smaller boats usually had just a husband and wife team, although often other family members, friends and even paid crew or paying guests had helped on some legs. The owners of the larger boats were usually assisted by paid crew, and sometimes these included experienced professionals who acted as skippers of the boat in all but name. Professional charter skippers ran five of the larger boats. The ocean sailor experiences the joys and the pressures of sailing at the extreme. However the challenges of an ocean voyage differ only in the degree from those of a holiday cruise in sheltered waters. Every weekend sailor will have experienced at least some of the problems faced by these skippers and crews.

The important practical lessons from this survey are interpreted in the light of additional information and anecdotes from my own medical and sailing experience. We asked both skippers and crew if they had been involved in any personality clashes or disciplinary problems during the voyage: 85 per cent of skippers and 71 per cent of crew answered yes. The slightly higher rating for the skippers is probably because they had on average sailed more legs and were more likely to have been aboard in port. We also asked if anyone had left the boat, or been ordered to leave it, because of personality or emotional clashes. With regard to this, we discovered that this had occurred on slightly over half of the boats. Such an end to the voyage was most common on the charter boats where the crew/guests were paying for berths.

Lord Nelson once said, 'It is ports that rot both ships and men.' Taking up this theme, we asked skippers and crew whether they felt that more clashes occurred in port or at sea. We discovered that 85 per cent of the skippers and 57 per cent of the crew believed that personal tensions and incompatibility were more likely to come to a head in port. At sea, the routine of the watch system provides a structure and discipline that is absent in port.

The first question from a non-sailor to an ocean voyager almost always concerns storms and gales, and there are gales and storms aplenty on the Southern Ocean route – particularly when rounding Cape Horn and the Cape of Good Hope. However, heavy weather is not usually a problem on a circumnavigation that passes through the Panama and Suez canals. The Europa race and almost all amateur yachtsmen follow this easier route. We asked about 'worst experiences'. The skippers talked of gear failure, financial problems or of personality and emotional clashes, but none of the skippers interviewed mentioned gales or storms in this context. The 'worst experiences' of the crew were more evenly divided. These included emotional and personality clashes, but some novice crew suffered considerable anxiety while handling the boat and during deck work, particularly at night and in the early stages. Not surprisingly, accidents or ill health were 'worst experiences' for the minority that were unfortunate enough to suffer such incidents.

When asked about tiredness, 85 per cent of skippers and 67 per cent of crew reported suffering from significant lethargy and fatigue. Participants were also questioned about a range of emotional and nervous symptoms; 77 per cent of skippers and 50 per cent of crew gave affirmative answers. The most common complaints were anxiety and depression. The level of distress was usually mild or moderate and often realistically related to specific problems. We judged the basic personality of the skippers to be in the main robust and stable. We attributed their higher level of tiredness and emotional distress mainly to the larger workload and the pressures acting on them. Most stresses were related to problems with gear, interpersonal problems with crew, and in some cases finance. Their symptoms were very similar to those that I have treated in overworked executives and managers. The skippers suffered from 'executive stress' – not 'sailing stress'.

Family crews

This is one of the most common and most successful arrangements for long distance cruising, and famous examples are the Hiscocks and the Smeetons. Many young couples are accompanied by their children, and older couples often have family as crew or take on an additional 'hand' for longer passages. The Europa survey confirmed that problems were least on boats crewed by couples or family. One adolescent daughter left after a row with her parents, but you do not have to go sailing for that to happen! Shared stress and danger generally strengthened relationships. A great strength of husband and wife crews was that where the marriage was stable, the couple had worked out a pattern of communication and a way of living together over many years. We asked the Europa crews to rate their skippers on a scale of 'good–average–bad'. Two wives when rating their husbands crossed out 'good' and wrote in 'excellent' – quite a tribute after 15 months at sea in a small boat.

We would advise a couple who are not confident about their ability to manage a long trip to be cautious about taking on a stranger as an extra crew member. This can be a recipe for rivalry and split leadership. The *Apollonia* tragedy (Chapter 4) provides an extreme example of this danger. Also, it is not easy for the extra person to live at close quarters with a couple on a boat that is also their 'home'. If you are reduced to this option, always take up references and spend some time with the person before committing yourself to an ocean crossing. The family crews seemed happiest when they sailed as a couple – perhaps with some assistance from friends or other family members well known to them. Stress was more likely when the couple felt that they could not cope alone and took on an extra crew primarily as another pair of hands. Two's company and three's a crowd, and this arrangement was often felt to be claustrophobic.

'Sell up and sail' is a common theme of yachting books and articles, but it is not something to be done in a rush. Retirement or redundancy, selling and moving house are in themselves stressful and disorientating experiences. Living aboard is very different from a holiday cruise. Long distance sailing inevitably entails separations, and women in particular find separation from family and friends, and the absence of their support, an important loss.

Living at close quarters also involves some loss of autonomy for both partners. We would advise a couple to spend some time adjusting to life aboard and gaining confidence before undertaking the additional stresses of an ocean crossing. Some crews and skippers experience quite high levels of anxiety and depression – occasionally to the point of a psychiatric illness that requires returning home for treatment. We felt that many of these stresses could have been reduced by a slower and more planned approach towards what is a considerable life upheaval. Difficulties were greatest where there were pre-existing strains or where one partner, usually the wife, was a reluctant sailor.

The couples that get on best often have clearly defined roles. One person is skipper and is usually almost entirely responsible for the boat and sailing decisions, while the other is responsible for the galley and domestic arrangements. This gives each person a degree of autonomy and thus reduces areas of potential conflict. This pattern may seem over-traditional and sexist, but the reality is that the man is usually – although not always, of course – the skipper. However, I have interviewed one couple where the woman was the very capable skipper and the man a contented 'househusband' – or whatever the nautical equivalent is.

Another important factor to consider is finance – particularly for older couples. It is easier to become a fancy-free sea gypsy at 20 than at 60. Worries about money, particularly if a house has been sold to finance the trip and there is no security to fall back on, can become a burden. Also, couples who have spent their life savings on a boat can easily develop expectations that are too high. An ocean passage is a wonderful experience, but it will not salvage a mediocre career or a failing marriage.

Charter berths

Chartering berths for transatlantic or ocean cruising has now become widespread. In many round the world races and rallies boats are quite often crewed by novices who have paid for their berth. For many this is their only opportunity of undertaking an ocean voyage, and for some the trip becomes 'the adventure of a lifetime'. Often, though, the trip is marred by tensions and ends in disappointment. Our Europa survey confirmed a very high incidence of emotional problems and personality clashes on the charter boats. We know of one charter boat that set out with six crew members, who had each paid almost £20,000 for the round the world voyage, and not one of the paying crew completed the circumnavigation. All had left or been 'put off' the boat! Some of the dissatisfied paying crew would have left earlier but for the fact that they had paid in advance and feared that they would lose their money.

Some charter boats are run on a shoestring, and owners desperate to fill

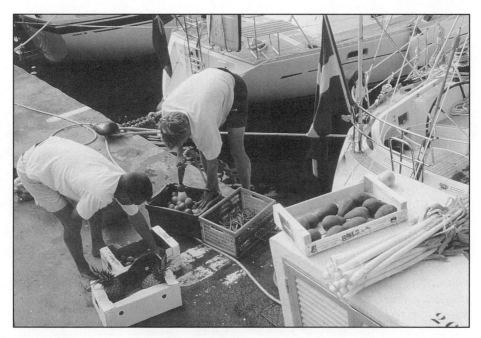

Loading up the boat with supplies. Preparation and planning in all areas is the key to a successful ocean crossing. PHOTO: *Jimmy Cornell.*

their berths are prepared to put to sea with novice crew who have not been through a proper selection process and have often never even met each other before departure. A professional skipper/owner and a 'mate' usually run a charter boat – the latter being responsible for cooking and for the organisation of the galley. These vessels combine the functions of a boat and a small, overcrowded boarding house.

Most of the professionals we met were excellent and experienced sailors, but had difficulty in dealing with tensions involving paying crew. One charter skipper told us: 'A lot of those paying for their berths have such antisocial habits that they couldn't expect anyone to be with them unless they were paying.' Yet there is another side to this equation, and subsequently two of the paying crew on this particular boat wrote to us to comment that: 'You pay... to be treated as cargo at sea and as a nuisance in harbour.' Port is certainly not an easy time on an overcrowded charter boat. The wife of one charter skipper wrote bitterly of 'having these strangers all over our home', and gave a party to which she invited those she liked and asked those she disliked to stay away. Clearly, this woman needed to remind herself of the fact that a charter boat with paying crew is not a home: it is a commercial enterprise.

What can be done to ease problems of this type? First, we would advise prospective paying crew to try to meet and assess the skipper and other crew to test out their compatibility. Secondly, the contract between the charter skipper and the paying crew, both at sea and in port, needs to be detailed and in writing. Also, be reluctant to commit yourself to a long voyage without first sailing on a short trip. Another point to be aware of is that ambiguity creates conflict: some guests expect to be waited upon while others are happy to pay in order to work. It is a great help if the crew have sufficient money to make some independent arrangements for travel and hotel stays while in port. Some charter guests we spoke to felt that this should be part of the agreement and be allowed for in the cost of the berth.

Not unexpectedly, there were many shipboard romances among the young, and sometimes not so young, participants. A shipboard romance is like an office romance, except that the 'office' is the size of a small corridor, has no soundproofing, and no one gets to go home! Most were fun and some ended happily. However, romantic and sexual relationships developing within small working groups tend to bring tensions and jealousies. A shipboard romance on a small boat affects everyone aboard, and several instances were recounted where the resulting tensions caused crew to leave.

World Cruising, the company that organised the ARC (Atlantic Rally for Cruisers) and Europa rallies, takes no responsibility for crewing arrangements. Nevertheless, this sort of cruising in company with other boats can give valuable support to crews. In spite of the clashes, we discovered that the atmosphere in ports was very festive and the organisers were supportive. Organised events gave the crews an opportunity to escape into a larger social group, and it meant that crews were able to change boats for both positive and negative reasons. Time and time again, it transpired that both charter guests and paid crew who found the atmosphere on one boat intolerable were happy on another vessel. There is safety in numbers and in a reputable organisation, and I would always advise a novice ocean sailor to try to join a boat in a major event, such as the ARC transatlantic rally or the BT Global Challenge. Organisers of events like these have learnt from a great deal of experience and now pay careful attention to crew selection and compatibility.

All the charter skippers that I have interviewed were capable and their boats were seaworthy. However, this is not always the case. I would advise any crew to take up references and to talk to past and present crew members. Some crew paying for berths on round the world yachts are buying the adventure of a lifetime, but many would-be trips to paradise are marred by tensions and misery and end in failure. Do not plan a voyage as a means of escaping from your troubles – they will surely follow you. Nor is it sensible to pay in advance for the whole of a world trip. Pay for one leg, or at most two legs, and wait and see how you get on.

Alcohol and drugs

We asked about alcohol in the Europa survey and 8 per cent of the race participants were felt by other crew members to be drinking sufficiently heavily to impair their efficiency. We were told an alarming story about an earlier ocean voyage during which the charter skipper had been overcome by stress and remained drunk in his cabin for days on end. It is obvious that heavy drinking, particularly by the skipper, may endanger the boat. Some skippers, including many racing skippers, run a 'dry' boat. There are advantages to this policy. In small quantities, alcohol relaxes, cheers and promotes sociability, but it also impairs concentration, judgement and co-ordination. In excess, alcohol may lead to quarrels and violence, and it is not sufficiently recognised that continual heavy drinking often results in depression. More than half a bottle of spirits daily is particularly likely to cause depression. Skippers are more at risk of this than the crew, and if someone becomes chronically depressed this possible cause should be considered. If excess alcohol is the cause of the depression, improvement will usually take place within a week of reducing alcohol consumption.

Most European countries have made it a criminal offence to drive with a blood alcohol level above a certain limit. In Great Britain this limit is 80 mgm per cent. This is a reasonable upper limit for sailing and allows for two full glasses of wine or the equivalent in spirits or beer. A person who had drunk more than this would carry a heavy moral, and even legal, responsibility if they were to make a mistake that resulted in injury or loss of life. It must always be remembered that no one is ever 'off duty' on an ocean voyage. 'All hands on deck' may be needed in an emergency at any time. Crew called from their bunks in heavy weather are particularly vulnerable to being washed overboard immediately on leaving the safety of the cabin. These obvious dangers will be increased if the person is confused and clumsy as a result of excess alcohol.

No one in the Europa survey admitted to, or reported, illicit drug abuse. My advice on drugs is straightforward. Do not allow on to a boat, or sail with, any person whom you suspect of carrying or habitually using illicit substances. There is a risk of disturbed behaviour from the drug taker, and other crew may find themselves innocently involved in serious criminal proceedings.

Episodes of confusion and psychosis may occasionally be precipitated by medication, including antihistamines, anti-seasickness tablets and anti-malarials. Should such an acute episode occur, it is best to stop taking any of these tablets. If medication is the cause, the problem will probably resolve itself within a matter of hours. Sedative medication – which includes anti-histamines and anti-seasickness pills – may cause drowsiness and clumsiness and can dangerously increase the effects of alcohol. Seasickness usually improves after a day or so at sea, but for some sailors it remains a continuing problem when the sea is rough; 30 per cent reported episodes of seasickness still occurring after 48 hours at sea.

Everyone knows that cigarettes contain the highly addictive drug nicotine. Tobacco smoke in the confines of a small boat is unpleasant and may exacerbate feelings of nausea and seasickness, so for good reasons smoking is banned on many boats. Some regular smokers have even put to sea without a supply of cigarettes in an attempt to force themselves to kick the habit. There are of course very good medical reasons for giving up smoking, but an ocean voyage in a small boat is not the place to try. The sudden withdrawal of nicotine results in craving, irritability, anxiety, insomnia and poor concentration, and these symptoms will not make you a pleasant and reliable companion and fellow crew member. By all means give up smoking, but it is only sensible to get over the worst of the withdrawal symptoms before putting to sea.

Medical factors and physical illness

We asked the 50 Europa participants in the survey about any medical or surgical problems that were serious enough to require hospital treatment. We also talked to one of the crew who was a qualified doctor and had acted as medical officer to the flotilla throughout the voyage. The problems encountered were stroke, serious leg injury, two crew who required abdominal operations for problems unrelated to sailing, a heart attack, and an episode of severe depression. One young crew member developed cerebral malaria and became seriously ill and comatose because of the failure of port doctors to diagnose his problem and treat him appropriately. Fortunately, he made a good recovery, but certainly this is a potentially fatal condition.

In addition to the usual run of minor injuries and illnesses, there were several problems with tropical ulcers in the Pacific – particularly the Marquesas Islands. It was there that the bite of a local sandfly produced unpleasant ulcers, which failed to heal even after oral antibiotics. The result was that several participants required hospital admission and intravenous antibiotics; and some infections took many weeks to clear up fully.

Seven participants were flown home, or to Western countries, for emergency hospital treatment. This high number reflects the fact that modern medical and surgical treatment is not always available at out-of-the-way cruising destinations, particularly in the Pacific islands. It cannot be overstressed that anyone embarking on a voyage of this type should take out adequate medical insurance cover that includes the full cost of air ambulance travel should that become necessary.

Detailed medical advice is beyond the scope of this chapter, but at the very least each potential crew member should have a full medical check-up before setting out on an ocean voyage. All boats should carry a medicine chest, a medical manual, and some means of radio communication so that clinical advice and intervention can be obtained. Recent advances in satellite and mobile telephone technology have made communication at sea easier and cheaper. I am aware of several examples of excellent medical advice being given by radiotelephone, which has enabled prompt and effective treatment of injuries and medical emergencies at sea.

On the Europa, as on the ARC rallies, the participants kept in contact daily by SSB radio. The participants always included doctors, who were able to give advice. These doctors were experienced and capable, and the fact that they themselves understood sailing conditions made their advice particularly appropriate and helpful. This is an important medical and safety factor offered by these rallies. Amateur radio networks are helpful in medical emergencies and have enabled specialist advice to be given on a worldwide basis.

Achievement

A list of medical and psychological factors and warnings can easily give too negative an impression. In spite of the stresses and financial costs, the most common emotional effect of accomplishing an ocean voyage in a small boat is a lasting sense of achievement and fulfilment. In this respect, the attitude of the Europa crews was typical. Most looked back with pride and believed that any hazards and difficulties had been well worthwhile; they had 'realised their dreams'. The husband and wife and family teams had a particularly high sense of achievement. Novice crew matured as sailors during the 14 months' voyage.

Not surprisingly, it was often the younger crew who had the greatest sense of personal development during the circumnavigation. Some had worked their way up the ladder from paying for a berth, to working their passage, to being paid crew – and even paid skipper. About half of the participants said they would do it again; many added that they would do it more slowly if they did do it again, and would spend more time in places that they particularly liked – such as the Pacific islands. Some crew experienced a sense of disorientation at the prospect of returning to 'normal life', and about half planned to undertake a further circumnavigation. One skipper spoke for many when he said that he would always guard closely 'the freedom to leave again'.

Sailing is a pastime that can be enjoyed throughout virtually one's entire life span. Families with young children, and even babies, seem happy and healthy at sea. Cruising children are generally content and well adjusted. Parental education seems to be effective, and most children return to normal schooling without disadvantage or difficulty. Whether at home or at sea,

Every landfall brings a sense of achievement. The author's boat Artemis *calmly anchored off Barbados after an Atlantic crossing.*

adolescents tend to find the constraints of the family irksome and feel the need to develop friendships among their peers. Their educational needs also become more advanced. For these reasons, most families find this an appropriate time to return to 'civilisation'.

Paid crew need to be young and fit, but many owner skippers and sailing couples are in their fifties and sixties. They have successful careers behind them and have accumulated the wealth needed to buy and run an ocean-going boat. The leadership and capacity they needed to succeed in their careers often stand them in good stead at sea. Successful men and women are usually good leaders, and hence potentially good skippers. Not everyone who makes a successful voyage is young and fit, however. One of the most remarkable achievements in the Europa was that of a 75-year-old woman who, having joined the rally as a paying crew, completed the circumnavigation serenely and cheerfully in spite of sustaining a very serious leg injury off Tahiti (a warp wrapped around her leg, cutting deeply into the calf muscle) and having to return to England for hospital treatment before rejoining the boat at Cairns, Australia. She had a good word for everyone and everyone had a good word for her. Afterwards, her ambition was to join a further charter rally and to complete the section that she had missed.

To would-be ocean voyagers I would advise: 'Do not jump in at the deep end'. A circumnavigation is still a formidable task even with modern equipment and communications. Try to ease the psychological pressures by making adequate financial arrangements and adjusting well in advance to such potentially upsetting life changes as retirement and separation from home, family and friends. Careful planning and preparation are essential.

Events like the popular ARC transatlantic crossing make an excellent introduction to ocean sailing. Prior to the November start of the ARC from Las Palmas, a week of seminars on ocean sailing are organised which are open to non-participants. These have provided an opportunity to learn and ask questions and also to share the excitement of the dozens of crews preparing for the start. To sail is to embark on a lifetime of learning – about the sea and about ourselves.

A Woman's Place is at the Helm

• Ros Hogbin •

The previous chapter considered some of the cruising aspects of contemporary long distance sailing by rally and charter crews, families and couples. Within this sphere today, there are numerous examples of women who sail and play a full part in crewing and on-board teamwork. Female skippers, however, have only comparatively recently established themselves on the racing circuit and in charge of cruising yachts. In this chapter, we look at how and why a small, highly motivated selection of such women have chosen to take this path, with reference to pioneering voyages and uncompromising racing challenges at the sharp end of the sport.

'The world of the seafarer is both a world unfit for ladies and one where women's presence leads to disaster... they are "the devil's ballast".' Thus ran the folklore of centuries past. 'They were not only weak, hysterical, and feckless and distracted the men from their duties, but they also brought bad luck to the ships they travelled in; they called forth supernatural winds that sank the vessels and drowned the men.'[1]

Even after such inauspicious beginnings, some women *did* manage to go to sea. There are records of a few female pirates, such as Anne Bonny, Mary Read and Grace O'Malley.[2] Women lived and worked on British Royal Navy ships, but they were hidden and their presence officially ignored. But as well as prostitutes and wives of warrant officers, some women actually served in naval crews, dressed in male disguise and under an assumed name. Once they had been found out though, they were dismissed. One such woman, 'William Brown', served as an able seaman in the Navy for over 12 years in the Napoleonic Wars and became a 'captain' of the topmen, skilled in working the sails, able to give orders, and gaining the respect of fellow seamen. She originally went to sea as a result of a quarrel with her husband about money.

It was not until well into the second half of the twentieth century, when yachting had developed sufficiently as a sport, that women in charge of their own boats began to make an appearance and embark on significant challenges.

Long distance pioneers

From an early age, Clare Francis was driven by adventure and dreamed of sailing away to far-off lands. As a young adult, on an impulse, she spent her legacy on a 32-footer, *Gulliver G*, and sailed across the Atlantic to win a bet. A two-handed round Britain race introduced her to long distance racing, which she loved. From there, the idea of taking part in a singlehanded race across the Atlantic, the 1976 OSTAR – dubbed by the press as 'the toughest race in the world... the last great struggle between one man and the sea... an impossible race in an improbable craft' – fired her imagination.

In her book *Come Hell or High Water*, she posed the question 'why?', realising that the main attraction for many was the very toughness of the race itself. But for her it was 'simply a great adventure in which you had to pit your wits and your skill against the sea. To go singlehanded was to add to the satisfaction and feeling of achievement.' She was not naturally a loner. 'Being alone would be a hardship that had to be endured, rather than a luxury to be enjoyed... there were risks of course... but many sports involve risk, and certainly an adventure is no adventure without it.'[3]

Even in the mid-1970s, the British attitude to racing in the OSTAR was still quaint and 'gentlemanly' – winning a race was not important 'unless by some delightful stroke of fate, one just happened to arrive first. But the racing mustn't interfere with the main purpose of the adventure, which was to have an enjoyable time in Plymouth, to make one's way across the Atlantic in a reasonably seamanlike manner without taking too long about it, and to have an even more delightful time in Newport by way of recovery.'[3]

Nonetheless, Clare Francis faced the realities of this gruelling race, 'the sheer misery of most of the voyage; the dripping damp, the terrible noise of the gales, the eternal fog, and the itchiness of a scalp covered in spikes...', coupled with loneliness, icebergs, 55-knot winds and 35-foot waves. As she reached the Grand Banks, she was struck by the terrible emptiness of it. 'I was aware of what I was – a small person in the middle of a large ocean. And it was a cold and lonely feeling.'[3] Clare Francis gave a very human portrayal of her joys and trials during the race on television, even allowing herself to show her vulnerability by crying on camera. She finished thirteenth overall, the first British monohull to cross the line and the first woman home, beating the record by three days. 'To sail an ocean singlehanded you need stubborn willpower and determination,'[4] she said. She would not be repeating the experience.

In 1977 Clare Francis went on to skipper *ADC Accutrac* in the second Whitbread Round the World Race, with a mixed crew, including her husband, Jacques Redon. Her time in the Southern Ocean prompted her to record a mixture of feelings: a horrifying terror of losing Jacques at sea, contentment and relief experienced in the aftermath of a gale, and the awe felt as force 10 winds blew: 'This is what we had come to find and sail through; this beautiful, powerful, magnificent ocean. As I watched I felt no fear, only simple admiration.'[4] Clare Francis was the first woman to skipper a Whitbread boat, finishing a creditable fifth out of 15.

Thus she completed the challenges she had chosen, at the boundaries of what was thought possible in the late 1970s. Her adventurous spirit and determination allowed her to succeed where few women had dared to sail before her. She blazed the trail and led the way for others to follow. Her sailing adventures, however, had come to an end. Yacht racing as a professional sport was in its infancy, and as yet very few sailors, let alone women, had carved out that particular niche for themselves. Clare Francis had already achieved what she wanted to achieve in sailing terms. She had no wish to strive for a long-term career in the sport; she was content to let her recollections fade with time.

Where Clare Francis had cast down the baton, Naomi James picked it up. As a child, she too dreamed of big adventures. She grew up on a remote dairy farm and admits to being shy as well as stubborn, liable to wander off, and fond of outdoor pursuits. 'I loved being outside on wild stormy days when the wind shrieked through the trees and the water poured down the valleys in heavy rain. I was fascinated by the elements and fancied it was because they were uncontrolled by man.'[5] A chance meeting with Rob James introduced her to the sailing life and to Chay Blyth, who was to provide her with the boat for her singlehanded voyage: 'I think what appealed to me about other singlehanded explorers was their aloneness. I sensed that there was strength in some people that was better expressed alone than with others and my instinct was to put myself in that category. My identification with their ability to function alone fed my confidence that such exploits were possible; if they could do it, why not me?'[6]

The possibility of a non-stop singlehanded voyage around the world excited her. 'It would be a commitment to myself alone, and if I were then to go back on the idea it would be a surrender I should find impossible to live with.'[5] 'It wasn't the sailing itself that attracted me in particular... I didn't really like sailing. What attracted me was the feeling, at sea, of wide open spaces. Choosing sailing was accidental; if Rob had been as committed a mountaineer, sky-diver, potholer – or whatever, I think I would have used that as a vehicle.'[6]

The motivation proved irrelevant. What counted was that Naomi James set off, as new to sailing as Chay Blyth had been when he first attempted to circle the globe: 'The physical challenges were at times considerable, but it was always possible to adapt, get around or brutalise myself to fit the occasion. I found the mental challenges less demanding because I found myself naturally suited to the environment... I didn't suffer much mental stress from the sort of intangible fears we have in our normal lives. Life was so practical on the boat; it was mostly a case of getting on with whatever transpired hour by hour.'[6]

Naomi James endured all the highs and lows that accompany a testing solo voyage around the world: lack of communications when her radio broke, feckless winds and slow progress, the loss of her cat overboard, navigational errors, and frustration in the aftermath of a storm. Finally, her self steering gear suffered irreparable damage, which necessitated a diversion to Cape Town to fix it, and ended the possibility of a non-stop voyage. '[I am out here] to prove that I am a rational, self-dependent and capable human being, one who has consciously chosen to try and live at the upper levels of man's capabilities and at the same time survive... The beauty of my life at sea alone is that my limits are the extent of my physical and psychological make-up. I succeed or fail by my own endeavours without any influence from the outside world.'[5]

At the end of her book *At One with the Sea*, Naomi James commented that the voyage enriched her life immeasurably: 'I hardly knew what I was saying... but I knew that what I was saying was important... That such an extreme endeavour was necessary at all is perhaps regrettable, but what I gained from it more than equalled the need I had to prove myself a competent and effective person.' [5]

Naomi James had become the first woman to circumnavigate alone: the pinnacle of her sailing career and an outstanding achievement for someone who didn't really like the sport! She did continue to race for a spell, but had no long-term sailing ambitions and, like Clare Francis, gave up soon afterwards. She said, 'I retired from sailing the moment I set foot on shore after the Round Britain and Ireland Race. I vowed I would never sail again and I never have.' [6]

Teamwork – a professional approach

In the same year that Naomi James undertook her epic voyage around the world, Tracy Edwards, the rebel child, and then only 16, left her family home and went to sea. Her contact with the yachting world signalled a turning point in her life. With self-opinion that erred towards the negative, coupled with a newly discovered determination to work in boats and reach the top, her attention focused on the Whitbread, by now a thoroughly competitive race, where women were still a rarity. This only added fuel to the fires of her ambition and she made it her business to take part in the 1985-6 race. She joined *Atlantic Privateer* as cook, describing the crew as the 'toughest, roughest racing yachtsmen in the world... The yacht's reputation was already a legend of male chauvinism and general squalor.'[7] One of the crew members told her she was bound to get off at the next port, which meant, naturally, that she completed the race!

'When I first thought of entering the Whitbread with an all-female crew it was because I wanted to give other women the chance I had craved so much. It was a dream, too, to achieve what so many had dubbed "impossible". '[7] Tracy Edwards had never skippered a boat before her Whitbread campaign, but she rose to the challenge, working intensively between 1986 and 1989 to find a crew, rebuild and prepare her boat, and raise money for the campaign.

Once the Whitbread began, with Edwards as both skipper and navigator, thoughts of winning were uppermost in her mind. The race provided her with a complete sense of fulfilment: '... total exhilaration; sheer joy at being alive and well, pleasure in everything around, love for everyone on board... How do you explain this feeling to anyone?... How do you capture it? It is one of the moments that everyone in the world deserves at least once.' Coupled with this were the inevitable lows: 'I feel like punching walls... I can't believe how pressured I feel. Exploding point is not far away.' And 'I have been terrified, ecstatic, depressed, confident, unsure, brave and cowardly.' Under Edwards' leadership, *Maiden* won two legs and came second in class overall. 'What I have ended up with is so much more than I could have hoped for. A new confidence, an inner strength and security.'[7]

Tracy Edwards' steely determination to succeed professionally marked her out as being fundamentally different to her predecessors. This ambition coincided with a racing career that began an important few years on from Naomi James's voyage. Far from leaving the sailing arena, therefore, Tracy Edwards further established herself as a professional skipper with her trademark female crew. She attempted the Jules Verne record in a 92-foot catamaran but was dismasted 2,000 miles from Chile, with the course uncompleted. She has gone on to develop her career as a presenter and motivational speaker, as well as considering new plans to compete in racing challenges of the future.

Cruisers with a difference

Sailing is a sport with many facets, and for some women the call of the sea is the call to cruise. Denise Evans skippered a boat and sailed with her sons when they were six, eight and ten. Later, she learned celestial navigation and cruised the Azores and the Caribbean chain. Approaching her sixtieth birthday in 1990, she undertook a challenging voyage with a mixed crew through the Magellan Straits and the Beagle Channel, and in 1998 she sailed to Greenland, taking a young crew with her. 'Persistence is better than talent,' she remarked, 'and I would include motivation in that. With motivation you can persist.'[8]

Anne Hammick, author of several sailing books, started to enjoy sailing as a teenager. She crossed the Atlantic, worked in the Caribbean, and crewed on an Atlantic delivery trip back to the United Kingdom. Aged 28, she skippered a Freedom 35 in the 1981 TWOSTAR, a two-handed transatlantic race, with her sister as crew, and went on to buy *Wrestler of Leigh*, a Rustler 31, which they sailed extensively together on several trips to the Caribbean and which Anne still owns and lives aboard in Falmouth. 'I moved on board in 1984 for our first long cruise in *Wrestler* and never got round to moving ashore again!'[9]

For Anna Brunyee, sailing took hold after a week with the Ocean Youth Club when she was 16; she worked her way up the ranks, eventually skippering a 72-foot ketch for them. By 1990 she was qualified as a Yachtmaster instructor and examiner and went on to buy the schooner *Mary Bryant*, undertaking skippered charters to the Caribbean, Iceland and Scotland: 'I enjoy cruising for the independence, freedom and self-reliance it affords... I'm just lucky to be able to do a job that I enjoy... I'm happy without much personal space or time, I'm interested in other people and enjoy hard work!'[10]

In her book *Maiden Voyage*, American Tania Aebi describes the single-handed circumnavigation that she began when she was just 18 and completed in two and a half years in a 26-foot yacht, spending 360 days alone at sea. She had a turbulent childhood and a restless, adventuring father, who determined that Tania should do something worthwhile with her life. The day of her departure was the first time she had ever handled a boat by herself: 'There was no-one to help me figure anything out, no-one to answer any of my thousands of questions, no-one to tell me if I had too much sail up.'[11]

A problem that haunted her for the entire voyage was that of heading out to sea alone: 'Psychologically, the first couple of days at sea were the most difficult to accept... it took me a while to adjust to the radically altered life condition. It felt almost impossible to slow down and swallow the sudden peace and quiet, as my mind worked overtime conjuring up navigational nightmares and weather worries... But as the days went by, my inner clock gradually slowed down. It was as if my metabolism eventually calmed and my thoughts were able to attain a degree of clarity difficult to achieve on land.'[11]

She crossed both the Pacific and Indian Oceans, battled her way up the Red Sea, and was knocked down in the Mediterranean. Finally, she crossed the Atlantic and arrived home: 'Now, in the same spot as I had been as an eighteen-year-old, setting off on her maiden voyage, scared and apprehensive of the future, I realised that the future wasn't something to worry about. If living at sea had taught me anything, it had revealed the importance of taking each new dawn in its stride and doing the best that I could with whatever was presented.'[11]

Challengers

As the range of sailing possibilities extended, so the opportunity to meet personal and racing challenges opened up worldwide. In June 1988 Kay Cottee became the first woman to sail solo, unassisted and non-stop round the world. She had sailed in Australia since childhood and had set up a boat-building and charter business, all the while developing her round the world ambition. One of her major concerns prior to the voyage was her state of mind while out at sea. So she consulted a sports psychologist, who took her through her fears: including hitting ice or containers, apprehensions about the weather, and pirate encounters.

As Cottee proceeded towards the halfway mark, she described her feelings: 'I love it out here by myself, no phones, no pressure, just a challenge to live with the elements everyday... for now I wouldn't swap places with anyone in the world.'[12] As her voyage continued, she returned from the tropics back into high latitudes and commented, 'It was just as well I loved the ocean in all its moods, otherwise I could have become very depressed with the black skies and gales in prospect for the next two months.' Moments of anger, frustration and pain did affect her. She also felt claustrophobic: 'plagued by shipping and hemmed in by land, even though the land was thousands of miles away on either side'. She suffered two knockdowns, 75-knot winds, and an extremely close encounter with a large steel structure, 'But the thought of giving in never crossed my mind – I was more determined than ever not to let the experience get the better of me.'

On her final approaches to Australia, Cottee felt deep sadness, so much so that before crossing the finish line she turned the boat round to escape for a short while, before completing the course and achieving her dream. As well as continuing to sail, she became a motivational speaker, raising substantial sums for charity.

One of the most challenging races, involving professional skippers and amateur crews, is Chay Blyth's BT Global Challenge, which takes place every four years. The inaugural race, the British Steel Challenge 1992–3, was the first of its kind to race identical steel boats round the world against the prevailing winds and currents. Of the ten skippers who took part, one was female. Vivien Cherry was a committed racing skipper, who found her own expectations and those of her crew differed: 'Because I am obsessed with sailing for sailing's sake, I had wrongly expected that most of the crew would share my feelings.' She felt the burden of motivating an amateur crew. 'Almost the only thing we all had in common was an avid keenness to do this voyage.'[13]

She fought on gamely during the race, accepting that she was a loner who found it difficult to understand her crew and finally admitting that single-handed racing in future seemed more attractive to her. Nonetheless, she skippered *Coopers & Lybrand* successfully round the world. Towards the end of the race, Cherry reflected that she had learned about motivation and team spirit the hard way – during a year instead of on a two-week intensive psychology course. 'Was it my hand of cards or the way I was playing them?' she asked herself, in an honest appraisal of her leadership. 'I think, in the end, it was the way I was playing them. There was nothing wrong with the cards I held.'[13]

Eight years later, the Millennium BT Global Challenge race saw two female skippers, Lin Parker and Alex Phillips, at the helm. With the experience of two successful races behind them, the Challenge Business had fine-tuned their requirements for 12 skippers, with a very thorough selection process, concentrating particularly on management and leadership skills. 'It was the toughest selection procedure I've ever been through for a job,'[14] Lin Parker explained, a woman who has sailed for more than 20 years and logged over 150,000 sea miles. Her upbringing in Zambia taught her independence and self-sufficiency and she was introduced to sailing via the ranks of the Ocean Youth Club. This experience, her work with a novice crew in the 1992 Round Britain and Ireland Race, and her Yachtmaster teaching and examining qualifications have equipped her well for the challenges she faces. She has a natural enthusiasm for the sport and an unspoken confidence in her own abilities, very much in harmony with the modern ethos, where gender is no longer an issue.

Alex Phillips also joined the Ocean Youth Club, which gave her a valuable grounding in a range of sailing skills. She studied yacht design and naval architecture at college, one of only two women in her year. She went on to teach sailing and discovered she enjoyed it, later becoming a training skipper for the BT Global Challenge, where 60 per cent of the crew join as complete novices. She is clear about the race: 'It's going to be the hardest thing I've ever done, without a doubt, but I think ever since I read *Swallows and Amazons...* it's been a subconscious ambition of mine, and my career's just generally led me down this path... The other huge benefit as far as I was concerned was sailing with amateur crews. It's just great to be able to help those guys achieve their goals.'[15]

Grand Prix racers: at the pinnacle of world-class racing

The 1990s saw the rise and further rise of the Grand Prix racer, competing in world-class events in Open 60s, or record-breaking multihulls. The French have been instrumental in setting up races and challenges such as the Route du Rhum, a classic transatlantic singlehanded race from St Malo to Guadeloupe, the Vendée Globe, a non-stop singlehanded round the world race which takes place once every four years, and the Jules Verne Trophy, a fully crewed non-stop round the world speed challenge, in which multihulls have succeeded in beating the original 80 day limit. They have also excelled in their provision of tough professional ocean racers, male and female alike. Three Frenchwomen – Arthaud, Autissier and Chabaud – have been at the forefront of development in this area.

Florence Arthaud was one of a group of navigators in 1984 to come up with the Jules Verne idea of circumnavigating the globe in under 80 days. Arthaud became president of the association that established the challenge. She won the 1990 Route du Rhum, came second in the 1996 Transat AG2R, took part on *Explorer* in the victorious Transpacific Yacht Race, and still has plans: 'I can't stand it when I'm not sailing,' she stated simply.

Isabelle Autissier started sailing to 'broaden her own character' and sailed alone because she didn't have the experience to sail on men's teams. Her racing credits are numerous, including the non-stop Vendée Globe, the longest singlehanded round the world BOC Challenge in 1990–1 and 1994–5, and the renamed Around Alone race in 1998–9. She was also guest tactician on *EF Education* for the last two legs of the 1997–8 Whitbread. In the 1994–5 BOC, she was dismasted in the Southern Ocean: 'I felt like I had been hit in the stomach. I thought "No. Not this. Not here"... But what was the use of yelling, shouting and crying in the southern mist for a victory that was completely lost?... I feel so much like crying for my lost hopes. But this is the way racing goes.'[16] Later, when her boat pitchpoled and rolled, she was rescued by the Australian military.

Before the 1998 Around Alone, Autissier reflected: 'Preparation for the race is mental... It is really difficult mentally, and less physically... Most of the work comes at the chart table... It's making sure that your calculations are correct, getting the boat into the right position and, most importantly, staying with the decisions you make.'[17] By the time she took part in the 1998 Around Alone race, she was contemplating her fifth rounding of Cape Horn, before another dramatic capsize west of the rock. Her boat *PRB* rolled completely and she was rescued by fellow competitor Giovanni Soldini. She had already decided that this would be her last singlehanded race around the globe, commenting that she had raced solo for about ten years, which was enough for her.

Catherine Chabaud has recently come to the fore as the first woman to complete the Vendée Globe Race (1996–7) and as overall winner on *Whirlpool Europe 2* in the 1999 Fastnet Race, taking the Fastnet Challenge Cup.

If it has taken Britain an inordinately long time to produce a world-class female singlehander, then Ellen MacArthur has been well worth the wait. Still barely in her mid-twenties, her life story and sailing progress are and will continue to be an inspiration for future generations of sailors. Her straightforward approach, personal drive and quiet enthusiasm for the sport ensure that she comes across as a major player in the global sailing stakes. This is

Ellen MacArthur – already a world-class singlehanded racing skipper by the age of 23. PHOTO: *Thierry Martinez.*

Below: Ellen MacArthur on board Kingfisher, *her Open 60 built in New Zealand for the Vendée Globe 2000.* PHOTO: *Thierry Martinez.*

backed up by solid, heavyweight sailing experience and a management team clearly focused on developing a long and fruitful career with her.

MacArthur was four when she first set foot on a sailing boat, and felt the excitement of it and the sense of adventure even then. As a child, she was an avid reader of all the sailing classics. By the time she was a teenager, she had cut her teeth on her second boat, a 27-foot cabin cruiser, which she refitted.

She then went down with glandular fever while studying for her 'A' levels: 'I remember watching the [Whitbread] trailer... and thinking "I'm not going to go to university." And it was like that – I'm going to sail. And that was it. I never looked back.'[18] She completely renovated a wrecked 21-foot Coribee while gaining her Yachtmaster qualification and teaching in a sailing school in Hull. Having won the 1994 BT/YJA Young Sailor of the Year award, with typical focus she thought: '"I'm going to sail around Great Britain" – It was as if I'd known it for years!' Aged just 18, she completed her lone voyage in five and a half months: 'I learnt about being alone and I learnt about me, about how I work... it's the time I grew up, because I was really pushed. It was hard. It was a tiny boat and there was a rush to get to the end.'[18]

With her sights firmly set on a career as a professional sailor, MacArthur competed in the Mini Transat, a tough transatlantic race in radical small boats. 'There aren't many people out there who understand singlehanded sailing and how it can feel sometimes... when you're with someone who's done it, they know and so when you say "it was pretty bad out there", you don't need to say anything else... You know that you would do anything that was required to help that person and you know that they would do that for you. And you need not even know them.'[18] She commented on the motivation needed when the wind dies away: 'You're in a race and there's a finish line to cross. And you know other competitors might have slightly more wind than you, so you have to work harder to keep up with them. You don't give up. You're frustrated and you want to cry but you don't give up. What would you do if you gave up?'

She went on to do a Round Britain and Ireland and won her class in the Route du Rhum. She prepared herself for her Vendée Globe entry with a punishing schedule of European and Atlantic races and the building and trialling of her new Open 60 *Kingfisher* in New Zealand, commenting: 'I think if you're someone who can spend time on your own, after you've done a transatlantic race, you know it. I know that the Vendée's going to be incredibly hard and lonelier than the other races that I've done, but it doesn't stop me wanting to do it... I want to make it happen.'[18]

Everything's possible

Although sailing has developed progressively as a sport from early in the twentieth century onwards, it was not until the mid-1970s that women really began to take their place at the helm, imbued with a sense of adventure and willing to step out beyond what had already been achieved.

In the short 25-year span since then, female skippers have led professional sailing teams in competitive races, cruised to far-off destinations, and taken their place in the challenges and world-class races of tomorrow. The twenty-first century looks bright both for the amateur and for the professional. Everything is possible. The challenge of the wind and waves remains the same for women and for men; the opportunities are there for those willing to grab them. As Ellen MacArthur says, 'You can make it happen!'

REFERENCES

1 *Female Tars, Women Aboard Ship in the Age of Sail*, Suzanne J Stark, Naval Institute Press, Annapolis, 1996.
2 *Bold in her Breeches, Women Pirates Across the Ages*, edited by Jo Stanley, Pandora, London, 1995 and San Francisco, 1996.
3 *Come Hell or High Water*, Clare Francis, Pelham Books, London, 1977.
4 *Come Wind or Weather*, Clare Francis, Pelham Books, London, 1978.
5 *At One with the Sea*, Naomi James, Hutchinson, London, 1979.
6 Naomi James written interview, February 2000.
7 *Maiden*, Tracy Edwards and Tim Madge, Simon & Schuster, London, 1990.
8 Lady Denise Evans telephone interview, April 2000.
9 Anne Hammick written interview, May 2000.
10 Anna Brunyee written interview, May 2000.
11 *Maiden Voyage*, Tania Aebi, with Bernadette Brennan, Hodder & Stoughton, London, 1989 and Simon & Schuster, New York, 1989.
12 *First Lady – A History-making Solo Voyage Around the World*, Kay Cottee, Pan, Sydney, 1989.
13 *Woman of Steel*, Vivien Cherry, with Keith Wheatley, Adlard Coles Nautical, London, 1993.
14 Lin Parker interview, May 2000.
15 Alex Phillips interview, May 2000.
16 *The Loneliest Race*, Paul Gelder, Adlard Coles Nautical, London, 1995.
17 Isabelle Autisser biography, Around Alone website, www.aroundalone.com.
18 Ellen MacArthur interview, January 2000.

The Bligh Mutinies

• Peter Noble •

We have analysed some of the qualities that combine to make a good skipper, so it is interesting to take a look at the career of the most infamous captain in British naval history: William Bligh. So deeply has the story of the *Bounty* mutiny etched itself in history that Bligh's name is now synonymous with tyrannical abuse. While Bligh's story is an extreme one, there are probably lessons here for all of us!

William Bligh was an able and moderately successful career officer who retired on a pension in 1813 with the rank of vice admiral. Most of us have heard of him only because of the events of a single night, the mutiny of Tuesday, 28 April 1789.

Yet the mutiny on the *Bounty*, which made him infamous, is but one in a series of similar incidents that continued throughout his career. The list of vessels on which his conduct gave rise to resentment, mutiny or near mutiny is long: the *Bounty*, the *Resource*, the *Director* and the *Warrior*. The story even continues to his deposition as Governor of New South Wales in 1808.

William Bligh's background

William Bligh was born near Plymouth on 9 September 1754, son of a customs officer. William's mother died when he was only 14, and by 15 he had enlisted as an able seaman-midshipman, which at that time was the standard entry for a potential officer. Between 1776 and 1780 he served as master of the *Resolution* on the last voyage of the explorer and navigator James Cook. There is no account of Bligh's conduct on this voyage, but by chance some evidence of his hypercritical attitude survives A fellow officer wrote a book about this voyage and a copy of this book in the National Maritime Museum at Greenwich is annotated with disparaging comments in Bligh's own hand!

In February 1781 Bligh married Elizabeth Betham – an intelligent and forceful woman from an influential family, who was in a position to help him in his career. Detailed information on Bligh's personal life outside the Navy is limited, and what little is known comes mainly from family letters, which speak of a happy family life and an affectionate relationship between Bligh and his wife and six daughters. If he *was* a domestic tyrant, then no complaints leaked to the outside world. His naval career was lived out against a conventional family background, with no clues as to what lay behind the extraordinary turmoil of Bligh's career.

Bligh's behaviour and demeanour as a naval officer from the time of the *Bounty* onwards is known in great detail from a number of primary sources, including many eyewitness accounts. Bligh himself published his own account of the mutiny and the subsequent voyage in the longboat. There are also court martial records, which

Captain Bligh. The small sailing boat in the background is the longboat on which he made a voyage of 3,500 miles. Courtesy of the National Maritime Museum, Greenwich.

include Bligh's court martial for the loss of the *Bounty* and the court martial of ten of the mutineers. The minutes of the subsequent courts martial in which Bligh was involved, directly or indirectly, are all available. Edward Christian, brother of Fletcher Christian, also published his own account of events, based on the testimonies of men who had sailed with Bligh. All this allows us to get to know Captain Bligh very well indeed – better than most historic figures, and better perhaps than some crew and skippers with whom we have sailed!

Fletcher Christian's background

Christian was 24 when he sailed with the *Bounty*. He was well educated and his family background was professional and minor gentry – a background not unlike that of Bligh himself. However, Christian had known much unhappiness in that his father had died when he was four and his mother was later bankrupted. Prior to joining the *Bounty*, he had sailed with Bligh on an earlier trip and been befriended by him. Some commentators have even suggested that a homosexual relationship existed between the two men and have tried to explain the later antagonism as a sort of lover's tiff. However, both Bligh and Christian were overtly heterosexual and there is no evidence of a clandestine relationship between them.

No letters or journals of Fletcher Christian have survived, and what we know of his personality and emotions comes from the accounts of his fellow sailors and the published record of his brother, Edward. While leading the mutiny Christian is reported to have cried out to Bligh: 'Sir, your abuse is so bad I cannot do my duty with any pleasure. I have been in hell for weeks with you.' Christian had become the object of Bligh's incessant criticism and their earlier friendship would have made that criticism harder to bear.

The voyage of the Bounty

The *Bounty* was a small, converted merchant vessel only 87 feet long. The purpose of her voyage was to gather breadfruit plants in Tahiti and then deliver them to the West Indies for cultivation. To achieve this, the ship had to be virtually converted into a floating vegetable garden in order to carry the plants, thus worsening the overcrowding of the crew. Clearly, it cannot be overstressed how powerful a factor overcrowding is in increasing conflict in both animal and human societies. The *Bounty* was too small to carry the usual detachment of marines, which could have been used to maintain discipline. Thus Bligh lacked any armed support when his authority was challenged. If marines had been on board it is highly unlikely that Fletcher Christian, whatever his grievances, would have dared to attempt a mutiny.

The *Bounty* left Spithead two days before Christmas 1787 and was soon lost to sight in the rain and spray of a rising south-westerly gale. Bligh, in a bad mood and blaming others, cursed the incompetence of the Admiralty, which had delayed his departure until this hostile and inappropriate month. His orders were to make all possible speed and to attempt a westerly rounding of Cape Horn against the prevailing winds. He was well aware of the dangers of Cape Horn, but would have kept these fears to himself. For many weeks the *Bounty* was battered by gales and repeatedly damaged as Bligh tried obsessively to follow orders under impossible conditions.

At this stage, there were no problems with the crew – danger alone does not lead to discontent. In fact, shared hardship often creates a sense of common purpose that sustains morale. It was not until April that Bligh finally abandoned the attempt to round the Horn and headed eastwards towards Cape Town on the longer and easier route to the Pacific.

Bligh was not the brutal and sadistic flogger shown in Hollywood epics. He was conscientious in protecting the health and comfort of his crew, and took measures to ensure adequate rest, dry clothing and a diet that prevented scurvy. It could be said that he showed a modern and politically correct concern for the proper treatment of indigenous peoples; and in Cape Town he criticised the slave owners' treatment of the black slaves for 'a want of decency and compassion in not relieving such a degree of wretchedness of which they were the cause'.

The *Bounty* eventually anchored in Matavi Bay, Tahiti, in October 1788. Bligh's instructions to his crew show a compassionate and sensitive attitude towards the Tahitians: 'Every person is to study the good will and esteem of the natives; to treat them with all kindness; and not to take from them by violent means, any thing that they may have stolen; no one is ever to fire but in defence of his life.'

When provisioning prior to departure from Tahiti, Christian's inexperience led to the loss of some equipment. Bligh immediately flew into one of his public rages, accusing Christian of incompetence and cowardice. Shortly afterwards, Bligh suspected that Christian and some of the crew had stolen several of his coconuts. He publicly abused Christian, calling him a thief and a scoundrel, and threatened to reduce the crew's rations as retribution. Clearly, this was not a prudent move – a hungry crew more easily becomes angry and disaffected.

The day after the coconut incident, Christian was in tears and talking wildly: 'He [Bligh] would probably break me, perhaps flog me and if he did it would be the death of us both, for I am sure I would take him in my arms and jump overboard with him.' Christian, in a state of extreme distress, even hinted at suicide and desertion: 'I would rather die ten thousand deaths than bear this treatment... flesh and blood cannot bear this.' Undoubtedly Bligh's bullying had stretched Christian to breaking point, and it is not surprising that Edward Christian, Fletcher's brother, should have blamed Bligh for his brother's desperate state of mind: 'What scurrilous abuse! What provoking insult... base, mean-minded wretch.'

The mutiny

By April 1789 the *Bounty*, loaded with a cargo of breadfruit, was sailing from Tahiti towards the West Indies. Bligh gives his own account of the mutiny in his journal: 'Just before sun-rising, while I was yet asleep, Mr Christian, with the master at arms, gunner's mate, and Thomas Birkett, seaman, came into my cabin, and seizing me, tied my hands with a cord behind my back, threatening me with instant death, if I spoke or made the least noise.'

The mutineers, led by Fletcher Christian, gained control of the ship, and Captain Bligh along with 18 crew who refused to join the mutiny were set adrift in the ship's 'longboat'. This open boat was only 23 feet long and 6 feet wide. It was propelled by two small sails and could also be rowed. It was overloaded, shipped water, and was only kept afloat by repeated bailing. Bligh was handed a sextant and navigational tables, but he had no chronometer. He was thus able to calculate latitude, his position north–south, but not longitude, his position east–west. Bligh's group had no firearms, so had little defence against hostile islanders.

Before setting off in the longboat Bligh confronted Christian and demanded to know if: 'This treatment was a proper return for the many instances [you have] received of my friendship.' Christian, in a state of obvious distress, replied: 'I am in hell. I am in hell.'

Bligh managed to land at the nearby island of Tofoa to take on board water and fresh supplies, but the inhabitants attacked the landing party and one of the seamen was killed. They then set sail for the nearest European settlement of Timor, which was in Dutch hands, a voyage of 3,500 miles in a small open boat. During parts of this voyage, they were attacked by natives in war canoes when they passed close to those Pacific islands that were inhabited.

The fate of the mutineers

Yet the situation of the 23 mutineers was no less perilous. They returned to Tahiti, a tropical paradise, which offered ample supplies, friendly islanders and accommodating women. However in choosing to remain and enjoy its delights they risked capture by a naval vessel and court martial.

The loyalties of the mutineers were divided. Some, including Christian, knew that capture and a return to Europe meant death. Others had been reluctant onlookers at the mutiny and had some hope of leniency. Not surprisingly, the mutineers split into two groups, with 14 choosing to remain on Tahiti. After only two years, the group that remained on Tahiti were arrested by the crew of HMS *Pandora*, which the Admiralty had sent to the Pacific in pursuit of the mutineers. The *Pandora* was shipwrecked on the return voyage and four of the mutineers were drowned. The ten surviving mutineers were charged with the capital offence of 'mutinously running away with the said armed vessel the *Bounty* and deserting from His Majesty's service'. Six were found guilty; of these, three were pardoned and three were publicly hanged.

Fletcher Christian, knowing that capture in the area of Tahiti was ultimately inevitable, had decided to set sail for Pitcairn, a remote and uninhabited island over 2,000 miles away. The *Bounty* reached Pitcairn on 15 January 1790. Aboard were eight mutineers, six Tahitian men, 12 women and a baby. Pitcairn was remote and difficult to access. The *Bounty*, which would have been impossible to conceal, was sunk off Pitcairn, where its remains have recently been discovered. There was no contact with the outside world for 18 years, until an American whaler landed at Pitcairn. The only surviving mutineer was John Adams. All the other mutineers and all the Tahitian men were dead – most had been murdered. The 35 inhabitants included the

Bligh being cast adrift from the Bounty. *A contemporary print by R Dodd. Courtesy of the National Maritime Museum, Greenwich.*

Tahitian women and their children, one of whom was Thursday October Christian, the 18-year-old son of Fletcher Christian.

The behaviour and fate of Fletcher Christian and his fellow mutineers was brutal. On Tahiti they had killed islanders in fights and raped and abducted their women. On Pitcairn, jealousy, sexual tensions and racism culminated in a series of murders. Around September 1793, the Tahitian men, whom the Europeans had treated almost as slaves, killed Fletcher Christian and other mutineers. Subsequently the Tahitian men were also killed – probably by the Tahitian women. John Adams was never brought to England to face trial, but allowed to live out his life on Pitcairn, which the descendants of the mutineers inhabit to this day. Adams gave varying accounts of Fletcher Christian's conduct, describing him as 'always sullen and morose... this mood however led him to many acts of cruelty and inhumanity... incurring the hatred and detestation of his companions here'. Of course it is possible that Adams criticised Christian in order to excuse his own actions, and in his latter years he took a more favourable view of him.

Near mutiny on the Resource

Bligh's career after the mutiny is a catalogue of conflict and acrimony between himself and his fellow officers. During the voyage in the longboat to Timor he failed to get along with his second-in-command, Fryer. Bligh was petty and over-critical, which in turn provoked increasing insubordination. At Timor, Bligh obtained a small schooner called *Resource* in order to continue the homeward voyage. But matters came to a head when *Resource* reached the Dutch colony of Surabaya, Indonesia on 12 September 1790. Fryer and the crew, some of whom were drunk, accused Bligh of using them 'damned ill'. There was a 'tumult' and threats of violence, which were only resolved when the Dutch authorities intervened on Bligh's behalf. The incident was a 'near mutiny' which stemmed from Bligh's failure to recognise and deal sensitively with petty grievances. If the *Resource* had been at sea, Bligh might well have been deposed for a second time.

Bligh sailed home to England without further mishap. He was court-martialled for the loss of the *Bounty*, but was exonerated – a verdict that was technically correct. Bligh's poor leadership had certainly contributed to the mutiny, but he was not criminally responsible.

Resentment on the Providence

In 1791 Bligh was put in command of the *Providence* and once again sent off to attempt to transport breadfruit from Tahiti to the West Indies. On this occasion, he took with him as first lieutenant his 26-year-old nephew, Edward Bond. Bond's position on the boat was the same as that held by Fletcher Christian on the *Bounty* three years earlier. Therefore we can make a comparison of Bligh's treatment of both Bond and Christian. Prior to this voyage, Bligh had a friendly relationship with Bond – just as he had had earlier with Christian. When writing to Bond, Bligh used his first name, Edward. Bond describes his uncle's style of leadership in the following terms:

> Hardly had the voyage commenced when Captain Bligh's arbitrary disposition and exasperating language began again to render his ship a most unfortunate one for his officers and especially for his First Lieutenant, who from disposition was brought into closer contact with him. Orders of an unusual nature were given with haste and in a manner so uncalled for and so devoid of feeling and tact as to occasion great irritation. A dictatorial insistence on trifles, everlasting fault-finding, slights shown in matters of common courtesy, strong and passionate condemnation of little errors of judgement – all these things tried the hearts of his subordinates and

worked them up to a state of wrath which would have probably surprised Bligh himself had he known it. In spite of the terrible lesson, which he already had in the *Bounty*, he appears by no means to have realised the state of wretchedness to which he reduced his officers.

Bond's account makes it quite clear that he had no objective grievance of any substance against Bligh. It was not a question of brutality or of seafaring incompetence: Bond's hostility was caused entirely by Bligh's style of leadership and personality, the relentless criticism, the lack of warmth, the failure to praise, and the failure to delegate. Bond was not in 'hell' like Christian, but Bligh's constant criticism had changed Bond's attitude from friendliness to rancour and resentment.

However, Bond was made of sterner stuff than Christian and was never brought close to breaking point. Strange as it may seem, Bligh was quite unaware of the hostility he aroused – he lacked insight. When the voyage was over, Bligh behaved in a friendly way towards his nephew and his correspondence indicates that he continued to help him in his career and wrote letters on his behalf in attempts to obtain promotion for him.

The voyages of the *Bounty* and the *Providence* are almost identical; and there are close parallels between Bligh's relationship with Christian and the later relationship with Bond. Not surprisingly, Bligh's continual criticism of both young officers turned affection into hatred and opposition: he had learned nothing from the lessons of the *Bounty*. This is demonstrated by Bligh's response to Edward Christian's explanation of his brother's behaviour: 'This sudden unpremeditated act of desperation and frenzy... a young man condemned to perpetual infamy, who, if he had served on board any other ship... might still have been an honour to his country, and a glory and comfort to his friends.' In replying to such accusations, Bligh is always at pains to stress his previous acts of affection and kindness to Christian and comments: 'He occupied the same place of confidence and trust to the moment of his horrid act of ingratitude.'

We could sum Bligh up by saying he was naive and emotionally unintelligent. He was not deliberately sadistic; he was just blissfully unaware of the distress and hatred that he produced in his subordinates.

Mutiny on the Director

By 1797 Britain was again at war and the fleet maintained a sea blockade of Continental ports. This was an unpopular duty, which involved tedious months 'on station' in all weathers. Discipline was harsh, and many conscripted crews were criminals or vagrants. Discontent increased until mutiny broke out and spread to over a hundred ships of the Home Fleet, stationed at

The Nore and Spithead. By this time Bligh had risen to the rank of captain and commanded the 64-gun *Director*, and for the second time in his career he had the indignity of being put off his ship by a mutinous crew. The Mutiny of The Nore, as it has come to be known, was a major threat to Britain's sea power. This time, the mutinous crews gradually surrendered, after confused negotiations and attempts at compromise. Most of the mutineers were never charged, but 36 of the ringleaders were court-martialled, convicted of mutiny, and hanged – a lenient outcome by the standards of the time.

The mutiny on Bligh's *Director* was only a small part of a more general mutiny involving discontented and mainly conscripted crew on many ships. It was a mutiny of the conscripted crew only. The officers, who usually got the worst of Bligh's tongue, were not involved this time, and for once Bligh's style of leadership cannot be blamed. The mutinies of The Nore and Spithead were of great historic importance, and for many months – during wartime – a substantial part of the fleet was out of action and England's defence was imperilled. Yet this story is little known to the general public, because it lacks 'human interest' when compared with the mutiny on the *Bounty*, a saga of conflict and tragedy.

Ill-feeling on the Warrior *and Bligh's second court martial*

Eventually the fleet returned to action, and Bligh continued with his naval career and fought at the battle of Camperdown in 1797, and Copenhagen in 1801. In 1804 Bligh took command of *Warrior*, a 74-gun ship of the line. But yet again he quickly clashed with one of his juniors, a Lieutenant Frasier. Bligh, forming judgements in his usual style, considered Frasier to be lazy and incompetent, and at a court martial he accused him of 'contumacy and disobedience'. Frasier was found not guilty and quickly turned the tables by accusing Bligh of misconduct. The evidence at Bligh's subsequent court martial throws further light on his style of leadership. Frasier alleged that Bligh: 'publickly on the quarter deck did... grossly insult and ill treat me... by calling me a rascal, scoundrel and shaking his fist in my face... he behaved himself towards me and other officers... in a tyrannical and oppressive and unofficerlike [way]... '

The *Warrior*'s officers gave evidence. Lieutenant Boyack described Bligh's abuse of his junior officers: '[Bligh's] expressions to his officers before the ship's company lessened their dignity as officers and were degrading in the extreme.' That Boyack, and so many junior officers, were prepared to risk their careers by testifying against Bligh – who held a senior and powerful position – is sure evidence of his deep unpopularity. The minutes of the *Warrior* court martial provide a long litany of Bligh's manner of addressing his officers: 'rascal and villain... rascal and scoundrel... audacious rascal... infamous scoundrel... dastardly villain... vagrant... thief... liar... God damn you... damn your blood... you damn long pelt of a bitch... you are a disgrace to the service...' It is clear that Bligh went on, and on, and on. Words – incessant insulting, critical words – ranted in public, will break more than bones. Such words will break a man's spirit.

The court found the charges 'part proved', and Bligh was reprimanded and admonished 'to be in future more correct in his language'. This court martial is important for the light it throws on Bligh's character and style of leadership. The abuse was particularly destructive because it was expressed in front of subordinates and because the victims had no immediate way of answering back. It was abuse like this that put Fletcher Christian into 'hell'.

Language in the eighteenth-century Navy was robust. Most recipients of this abuse endured in silence and continued to perform their duties: Bond got it out of his system by writing his feelings down in his diary; Frasier waited until he returned to England and then defeated his tormentor at a court martial. Only the vulnerable Fletcher Christian was pushed to the edge of a nervous breakdown and disaster.

Another acrimonious voyage

Yet the 'admonition' of the court had not the slightest effect on Bligh's style of leadership. He was appointed Governor of New South Wales and in February 1806 set sail for Australia in a small convoy, sharing joint command with a Captain Short. A joint command with the possibility of split responsibility is a potential recipe for disaster, and the two captains were quickly at loggerheads. In one incident, the enraged Short even fired shots across the bows of Bligh's ship. After arrival at Cape Town, both sides poured out their grievances to Francis Beaufort (inventor of the Beaufort scale, still used in weather forecasting). His account of the meeting criticised both men: 'they were both wrong, both had acted intemperately and foolishly, both had laid themselves open to censure... both are equally resolved to stick to what they had already done and not to retract a single word'. And then added: 'one [Bligh] was a man of talent the other was an ass'.

Mutiny in New South Wales

In 1806 New South Wales was an agricultural settlement and penal colony around Sydney Harbour. Once he arrived in Sydney, Bligh became Governor and power then lay in his hands, and he used his power of office to indict Short before a court of enquiry and force him to return to England with his

Bligh's last mutiny. While Governor of New South Wales, Bligh was dragged from under his bed and arrested by his own militia. Courtesy of the State Library, New South Wales.

pregnant wife, who died on the journey. On return to England, Short was court-martialled, but acquitted and awarded compensation.

From the beginning, Bligh's tenure as Governor was marked by rancour and conflict. The colony was in a poor state, and settlers, ex-convicts and convict labour carried out farming on recently cleared land around Sydney. Law and order was the responsibility of the New South Wales Corps, a militia of 400 men. But the militia was corrupt and its officers improperly enriched themselves by grants of land and a monopoly of the barter of rum. Any attempt by a new governor to curtail these corrupt but lucrative privileges would inevitably give rise to resentment.

Bligh weakened his own moral position by accepting a grant of land from the previous Governor in return for favours, and he soon alienated powerful and influential settlers and the militia, on whom he depended to enforce his authority. His leadership style as Governor had not changed from when he was a sea captain. He was arrogant and abusive in a situation that demanded tact and judgement.

After two years of rising discontent, matters came to a head and Bligh faced his last mutiny. The militia, in dress uniform and band playing, marched on Government House and Bligh was deposed and placed under house arrest. It was alleged, although Bligh himself denied it, that he was found trying to hide under his bed and was dragged out by his own militia. He remained under arrest for a year until he contrived to get himself aboard the naval vessel HMS *Purpoise*, which had remained in the area but had taken no part in the conflict. Once aboard *Purpoise*, Bligh used his naval rank to assume command. *Purpoise* spent a year sailing back and forth between Sydney and Tasmania and, once more, Bligh made life unpleasant for his fellow officers. All parties involved in the dispute sent self-justificatory letters to London. Mail was slow in the days of sailing ships and it was not until May 1809 that Lachlen Macquarie was appointed to replace Bligh.

The New South Wales mutineers fared better than did their predecessors on the *Bounty*. Only one person, Major George Johnston, was charged with mutiny. He was convicted and sacked, but was not otherwise punished. The authorities clearly believed that the incident was the result of mismanagement and provocation. At this point, Bligh returned to England; the Admiralty promoted him, but never again gave him an active command.

Bligh died in London in 1817 and was buried at Lambeth. His tombstone chronicles his achievements, but makes no mention of the *Bounty* or of the governorship of New South Wales.

Bligh's qualities as a leader

There has never been any serious criticism of Bligh's technical competence. He was an intelligent man, an excellent navigator, and a capable sea captain. And there is no evidence of physical cruelty. He was not a sadistic flogger; on the contrary, he was painstaking in his concern for the safety and comfort of his crew. His attitude to indigenous peoples was enlightened and modern, and he had immense experience as a navigator and of warfare at sea. His determination and physical courage were redoubtable. Yet in spite of all these considerable virtues, his name has become synonymous with abuse and cruelty.

The problem with Bligh's leadership was what he said and the way in which he said it. His officers were subjected to repeated criticism over petty matters, and this criticism took the form of tactless public abuse. He did not trust his subordinates, had difficulty in delegating, and continually interfered. He rarely praised or encouraged. Psychologists have dubbed this very ineffective style of leadership 'negativism'. Bligh was quite unaware of the effect of his conduct on others; he lacked 'emotional intelligence', which involves sensitivity to the feelings and expectations of others. He was completely surprised by the *Bounty* mutiny and never guessed that his criticisms had reduced Fletcher Christian to a state of rage and despair.

Bligh also showed an extraordinary inability to learn anything from his mistakes. On the *Providence* he was quite unaware of the resentment that his behaviour produced in his nephew Edward Bond. Bligh was rigid and obsessive, which may be good qualities in a navigator, but hamper a leader who needs to delegate and to make allowances for human frailty. Bligh neither trusted nor delegated. He wrote of the competence of his fellow officers: 'As to the officers I have no resource, nor do I even feel myself safe in the few instances that I trust them.' He was constant in his virtues and defects: his style of leadership as Governor of New South Wales repeated that as Captain of the *Bounty* at the beginning of his career.

Bligh's style of interaction contained almost all the defects that modern psychological and military studies show to be associated with poor leadership and poor morale among those who are being led. The epithet 'Captain Bligh' has a historic basis but it is still applied today to a skipper who is domineering, over-critical and foul-mouthed. But Bligh's defects were matched by equal virtues, and in researching this chapter I feel that I have got to know him very well from the many first-hand accounts. My own attitude to him is summed up by George Tobin, who served under Bligh, and responded to learning of his death with the words: 'So poor Bligh, for with all his infirmities... I cannot but think well of him.' I have met several modern 'Captain Blighs' – but none with the courage, seamanship, navigational skills and determination of the original.

REFERENCES

Allen, Kenneth S, *That Bounty Bastard: The True Story of Captain William Bligh*, Robert Hale, London, 1976 and St Martin's Press, New York, 1977.

Bligh, William, *A Book of the 'Bounty'*, edited by George Mackaness, EP Dutton, New York, 1938.

Christian, Edward, *Minutes of the Proceedings on the Court Martial, held at Portsmouth, 12 August 1792, on Ten Persons charged with Mutiny on Board His Majesty's Ship the 'Bounty', with an Appendix containing a full Account of the Real Causes, etc.*, London, 1794.

Dening, Greg, *Mr Bligh's Bad Language: Passion, Power and Theatre on the Bounty*, Cambridge University Press, Cambridge and New York, 1992.

Kennedy, Gavin, *Captain Bligh: The Man and His Mutinies*, Duckworth, London, 1989.

Getting on Together: Crew Compatability

• Peter Noble •

Sailing can be an enjoyable and life-enhancing pastime: most sailors are physically and emotionally robust and sailing helps them to stay that way. However, the stresses and confinements of sailing can produce emotional problems and conflicts in many crews. Even a weekend sailing trip can be ruined if there is tension or ill-feeling aboard. It is probably fair to say that personal tensions have spoiled more sailing holidays than heavy weather.

Of course, the experience of crews in round the world races is much more extreme than weekend or holiday sailing, and has been extensively reported in books and articles. In some boats, very severe tensions and conflicts have developed, whereby crews have split into warring factions. Most difficulties can be sorted out, but in some cases emotional problems may impair the efficient running of the boat and certainly lessen the pleasures of the voyage. Obviously the skipper carries the greatest responsibility and thus faces the greatest stress – some skippers have become so unpopular that they have faced mutiny or been sacked by their sponsors.

Prolonged physical discomfort and overcrowding undoubtedly increase stress and personality conflicts, but clearly there are certain factors that promote harmony and effectiveness on a boat, and others that increase the effects of stress and may lead to inefficiency, exhaustion and even mental breakdown.This chapter looks at lessons learned from scientific research into this matter, and interprets the information in the light of my own experiences as a yachtsman and as a psychiatrist.

Stress, sleep deprivation and exhaustion

Fatigue and lack of sleep impair concentration and decision-making. This is why there are laws to regulate the number of hours at a stretch that a bus driver spends at the wheel or a civil pilot has charge of an aircraft. A skipper and crew on a yacht at sea have to impose their own restrictions; there are no laws that will provide them with a respite if they become exhausted. However, there is much that a wise skipper can do to protect himself and his crew. Most studies of the effects of the extremes of sleep deprivation and exhaustion on performance have been carried out on combat air crew, sailors and soldiers. Clearly, there are no statutory rest breaks in the middle of a battle. Knowledge of these effects is of obvious importance for service commanders.

The results are clear cut. The subjects usually continue to be efficient in purely physical tasks in which they have been well trained even when pushed to the limits of physical exhaustion. A deterioration in competence in physical tasks does occur, but this is a slow process. This fits with what we know of long distance sailing. For instance, I would expect an experienced skipper or crew to be able to take down the main in a rising gale and perform the task competently and safely in spite of days of sleeplessness and exhaustion. And this is why singlehanded sailing in the open ocean is less hazardous than it might appear. Ocean sailing, particularly in heavy weather, often means hard physical work, but psychological or mental tasks become more important as land approaches. When you are tired you can recover your physical skills fairly quickly – even half an hour's catnap is beneficial. The most exhausting time that I have ever lived through was not on a boat but as a junior doctor. I survived nights on duty without sleep by learning to take catnaps at any time of the day or night and whenever the opportunity presented itself – not the ideal way to practise medicine, but an excellent training for shorthanded sailing.

In contrast, the ability to perform psychological/mental tasks quickly deteriorates as exhaustion increases, and sleep deprivation and overtiredness impair judgement and problem-solving. There is a tendency in this state to take uncharacteristic risks, decision-making becomes poor, and tasks are neglected. A vessel close to land or reefs may be endangered simply through the mental exhaustion of her crew and skipper. Fear and seasickness are also debilitating, and further increase fatigue.

Such a deterioration is insidious and often the person concerned does not appreciate that they have been reduced to incompetence; insight is lacking. There are many stories of shorthanded yachts crossing oceans safely only to be wrecked close to land because of some elementary error of navigation. After the loss of his boat *Smew*, Edward Nott-Bower wrote: 'It is difficult to trace the exact stages by which one is transmuted from a reasonably energetic and companionable person at sea to a silent slow moving being... clogged with heavy lassitude whose every thought and movement demand a conscious effort of will.'

Even in heavy weather it is safer to heave-to and rest in open water than to attempt to close the land – particularly at night. It is important that the skipper does not become so anxious that he neglects to rest, and a good watch-keeping rota is an obvious safety factor in this (see page 56). To misquote John Wayne:

Preparation reduces stress. The mainsail is taken down in good time before a rising Atlantic gale – the author's yacht Artemis.

'When the going gets tough the tough lie down.' When sailing in difficult conditions nothing is more reassuring than noting that the off-watch crew are tucked up and asleep – they will then be fresh when their turn comes.

In difficult situations calm and confident leadership is important, but of course this is easier said than done. As we have seen, a common fault among inexperienced skippers is to try to do too much themselves: it is essential to think ahead and to delegate. Even a novice crew can keep a lookout in bad weather, which is often all that is required. Good skippers give priority to keeping the watch system working, and to getting some rest themselves whenever the opportunity arises. An exhausted skipper soon becomes an incompetent and poor leader.

Emotional breakdown under physical stress and danger

A review of 25 scientific studies lists the factors that relate to breakdown in air crews during combat. Role confusion and lack of training as a team increase stress and the risk of breakdown. And factors such as fatigue, hunger, cold and sleep deprivation lower morale and reduce resistance to hardship and danger. On the other hand, good leadership, group cohesion and 'esprit de corps' are protective.

It is not being suggested that sailing is a form of combat, but any experienced sailor will recognise that this list, based on air crew research, has a close application to crew morale when sailing in difficult conditions. Good leadership by the skipper reduces the stresses acting on the crew. Role confusion and lack of training have the opposite effect. A good skipper considers the emotional needs of the crew when taking decisions, not just technical factors.

The sea cannot be controlled, but careful preparation and mutual help can lessen the stress of difficult situations. For instance, a seasick person often becomes too debilitated to move from the cockpit and huddles there ill, wet and increasingly cold and dehydrated – a danger to themselves and a nuisance to others. They must be helped to a warm berth and encouraged to take fluid and food. A combination of inexperience, fear, exhaustion and seasickness is particularly dangerous. Lifeboatmen frequently report that rescued crews are in a state of total collapse, even in moderate conditions. Often the watch system quickly breaks down when a badly led and inexperienced crew face difficult conditions. Everyone becomes exhausted to no purpose, and no one is able to rest and recuperate. The preparation of meals and self-care are neglected and the crew rapidly become cold, hungry and dehydrated. All this can be reduced, or even totally prevented, by good preparation and leadership.

Yacht design is important in reducing stress. The traditional, heavier, long-keeled yacht is more comfortable in rough seas and will more easily heave-to or lie a'hull. Hence a seaworthy and seakindly boat reduces fear and discomfort when sailing in heavy weather. One of the many pleasures of sailing in *Artemis*, my Peter Brett-designed Rival 34, was that in storm conditions the boat looked after itself and the crew concentrated on looking after each other. Of course, amateur crews have made successful and fast ocean passages in modern light displacement boats, but be warned that these boats are uncomfortable and difficult to sail in rough seas. The safety margins, particularly for an inexperienced family crew, are lower.

Almost every boat has a first aid kit and a medical manual that gives advice on how to deal with medical emergencies such as appendicitis, coma or serious injury. Fortunately, such emergencies are very rare and most of us will not come across such situations in a lifetime of sailing. But just as important as treating physical emergencies is being able to intervene sensibly and effectively if psychological problems occur. Occasionally a stress reaction develops and this can take various forms. It is usually caused by the pressures of confinement, exhaustion, seasickness and fear. Such reactions are very uncommon on a 'happy ship', unless of course the sufferer already has a history of psychological problems. Symptoms may include anxiety, depression, lethargy, hostility, inefficiency and an inability to carry out ordinary duties. Ideally the situation should be recognised at an early stage and before the person reaches a state of collapse. You do not have to be a doctor or a psychiatrist to help. The following advice, which is based on many studies in military medicine, is easy to apply on board:

- Allow at least a day of complete rest and withdrawal from all duties. Try to make the person as comfortable as possible.
- Do not criticise, blame or bully. Be reassuring – recovery is usually fairly prompt.
- Special medication is not necessary. If there is severe insomnia, some sedation at night may help. Use what is available on the boat – such as a double dose of antihistamine or anti-seasickness tablets, or a drink of warm milk and brandy.

Emotional and personal problems developing in small craft

The most extreme example of small groups living and working together for prolonged periods in cramped and hazardous conditions is space exploration. For example the Russian *Salyut 6* space programme required that cosmonauts live and work on a space station for periods from several months to over a year. All the cosmonauts were young, fit and emotionally stable – which is rather more than can be said of the average cruising skipper! All the cosmonauts had superb technical skills but, even so, tensions and stresses developed among the crews as the space programme progressed. Increasing attention had to be paid to mutual compatibility and interpersonal problems. The Russian psychologists studying the cosmonauts found that the best prediction of 'crew compatibility' was to study past experiences, and potential crews were observed and tested while living and working closely together. For instance, trainee crews were required to undertake car journeys lasting several days, whereby the crews spent the entire time cooped up together apart from brief scheduled stops for fuel, provisions and the disposal of waste. Trainees who developed tensions under these claustrophobic circumstances were transferred to other programmes. So it seems that if you really want to predict how you and your crew will get on together, buy yourself a Lada (much cheaper than a yacht), cram them all in together, and spend a week with them driving back and forth – preferably across Siberia! If at the end of that week no one has been throttled and you are all on reasonably good terms, you will probably be fine on even the longest and most difficult ocean crossing.

On a more serious note, though, I am very concerned by the extent to which sailors who sometimes have not even met, and have not been through any sort of selection/compatibility procedure, are prepared to commit themselves to long ocean voyages. Not surprisingly, in these instances there are significant levels of stress and the drop-out rate is high. Even a brief meeting with someone you intend to sail with has a limited value. For example, there really is such a thing as 'taking an instant dislike' to someone. It is a most unpleasant feeling and rarely improves by living with that person at close quarters. Ideally, the crew should make a preliminary voyage together, before setting off on a longer passage. And certainly the 'shakedown' cruise from southern Europe to the Canaries is a good predictor for the longer Atlantic crossing. If it really isn't possible to sail together, then it will be very helpful to spend some time ashore in each other's company. For instance, a long weekend in a small country cottage will provide helpful information about temperament and compatibility.

Adverse reactions observed on prolonged space missions include tiredness, lethargy, irritability, emotional instability, insomnia and interpersonal tensions and conflicts, and these increase the longer the duration of the mission. Charter skippers recognise that most crews can manage to get along together for a week; it is longer voyages that are likely to give rise to difficulty. Once again, well-organised schedules with specific periods for work, leisure and social activities and sleep are extremely important in order to minimise problems.

Watch-keeping and shipboard routine

The importance of a well-run watch-keeping system cannot be over-emphasised. It is important for morale as well as for safety. It is best for crew to know well ahead when they will be on watch and when their time is their own. This enables each person to organise his or her own timetable of sleep and activity and allows the off-duty crew to rest without a feeling of guilt. If crew numbers permit, there is much to be said for a system where the skipper is not part of the watch system, although inevitably the skipper will always be on call. Most skippers do not delegate sufficiently and tend to overtire themselves, and this results in loss of efficiency.

A watch and duty rota is important even on a short sail of a few hours. With a crew of only two on an ocean voyage, time off watch does not need planning – most of it will be spent asleep. For a larger crew, who are not racing, there is often a considerable time off watch, and there is a temptation to spend long hours unoccupied and in a rather drowsy and lethargic state. Mild seasickness may contribute to this. Evidence from the studies of the Russian cosmonauts found that morale was improved and stress reduced by organised off-duty leisure activities. When I am sailing long distances I always make an off-watch timetable for myself and allot regular times for boat maintenance, navigation and reading. This helps me to feel more awake when out of my bunk and to sleep better when in it.

Small groups have been shown to work most effectively where they have some sense of autonomy and the ability to monitor their own standards. It helps a sense of involvement if the duty watch have the authority to allocate tasks among themselves and to take some responsibility for course changes, sail setting and navigation. It also helps morale if the skipper is able to discuss decisions, delegate and supervise unobtrusively; if popular and unpopular tasks are not fairly distributed, the skipper has a duty to intervene early before chronic resentment develops.

Humans are territorial animals and, as already mentioned, tension and aggression increase with overcrowding. Therefore, the potential emotional problems of overcrowding are important when deciding crew numbers. If space does not permit crew to have their own cabin, or even bunk, there must be some fair distribution of stowage space which is not then intruded upon by others. Mutual tact allows the development of some psychological space despite physical overcrowding, for example tidyness and the careful stowage of personal gear shows consideration for others. Good crew are self-contained and non-intrusive. There are times for sociability, but it is also important to respect the privacy of others and to erect the nautical equivalent of what, in the City, is known as a 'Chinese wall'. A crew is a family, and as George Bernard Shaw wrote: 'A family without manners is impossible... it can only be kept intact if all parties behave with the most scrupulous consideration for one another.'

Sailing should be fun, and the skipper must do his best to ensure that the crew can relax and enjoy themselves. There may be tough times, but a well-led crew can build on these to enhance morale and team spirit; a difficulty or danger surmounted is life-enhancing. A 'happy hour' when all the crew can meet together for a drink and discuss any problems helps to build teamwork and diffuse tension. On long trips on my own boat, *Artemis*, the 'happy hour' was so successful that I instituted *two* 'happy hours', one at 12 noon and the other at 6 pm!

If there is not a regular cook on board, the galley arrangements can become another source of tension and conflict. Cooking at sea is important, but is also sometimes difficult. With large crews, a rota system whereby the 'cook for the day' is excused all other duties often works well.

The boat must be adequately provisioned and the crew well fed. It should be clear what are 'ship's stores' and reserved for the cook's use, and what provisions are available for everyone's casual use. It is really important that there should be some additional foodstuffs/beverages so that the crew can feel free to make themselves a cup of tea or have a snack. On his famous Arctic voyages, Tilman carried indigestible black bread on the grounds that the crew did not like eating it and thus saved on cost and storage space. He made some outstanding passages, but few sailed with him twice!

Crewing on a yacht inevitably involves the surrender of much privacy, autonomy and control, so do not exacerbate this problem by planning too rigidly. One skipper on the ARC transatlantic rally told me the sad story of his fruitcakes. Each small cake was exactly the right size to be cut into five slices – one slice for each of the five crew at elevenses. He had planned and provisioned for exactly one fruitcake per day. One young crew member would always ask for a second slice, which put out all the calculations. The skipper bit his lower lip in silent rage from Gibraltar to Las Palmas, where he promptly put the 'offender' off the boat.

Preparation is all-important. Much of the work that needs to be done to promote harmony should be in place before the boat leaves port:

- Crew selection is essential – temperamental incompatibilities should be discovered early. It is better to sail shorthanded than to take an unreliable crew or a potential troublemaker.
- Arrangements for stowage, berths and provisioning all need careful thought. My own preference is to sail shorthanded, rather than be over-crowded. A successful modern skipper must be able to discuss key issues with the crew.
- Galley and cooking arrangements are too important to be left to chance. Cooking at sea is more difficult than navigation and just as important.
- There is no perfect watch system; it is a matter of what best suits the conditions and the crew. However, it is something that needs to be thought about and discussed before setting sail. I have sailed happily under many watch arrangements, but I have never sailed happily on a boat where the watch system was not clear and well organised.

Each crew is a different and unique community, and some yachts are happier than others. On a few vessels, stress and discord impair enjoyment and lessen efficiency and safety. In reality, there are no set rules and no set advice. Nevertheless, there are many lessons to be learned from the scientific studies

Running under bare poles before an Atlantic gale – the author's yacht Artemis.
A watch is kept, but the crew are warm and comfortable below.

of air crew and military personnel who have to function as a team in hazardous and overcrowded conditions. Attention to these lessons will increase the chances of making a successful voyage with a happy crew.

REFERENCES

Kanas, N, 'Psychosocial support for cosmonauts', *Aviation, Space and Environmental Medicine*, 1991, pp 353–6.

Lamberg, L, 'Effects of sleep deprivation on performance', *Sleep*, 1996, pp 318–26.

Leach, J, 'Psychological first-aid: a practical aide-mémoire', *Aviation, Space and Environmental Medicine*, 1995, pp 668–74.

Santy, P A, et al, 'Multicultural factors in the space environment: Results of Shuttle crew debriefing', *Aviation, Space and Environmental Medicine*, 1993, pp 196–200.

Talka, N F, Koffman, R, Bailey, D A, 'Combat stress, combat fatigue and psychiatric disability in aircrew: a review', *Aviation, Space and Environmental Medicine*, 1994, pp 858–65.

The *Apollonia* Tragedy

• Oliver Wall and Peter Noble •

We have looked at the importance of skipper/crew compatibility; here is an account of extreme incompatibility – resulting in a double murder.

If you were to stand on the dock at any port where yachtsmen make their landfall after several weeks at sea, you would certainly hear some tales. Once the feeling of achievement has worn off, a crew often splits up, with varying degrees of relief at being released from the hothouse atmosphere of a small vessel. Crew often join boats they know nothing about to sail with skippers who may be incompetent – even predatory. Likewise, owners can spend years and years planning a cruise – the boat, the equipment, the weather, the route – yet, despite such painstaking preparations, they may take on crew they barely know, without a trial passage or even a recommendation.

This tragedy happened on a voyage between the Canary Islands and Barbados, when the skipper of a German yacht took on four crew from the dockside. What follows is an account of a voyage that went terribly wrong, and an explanation of how the situation developed and of how it might have been avoided. This story is an extreme event, a so-called worst-case scenario. As we have already seen, the selection of crew, the skipper's leadership and the patterns of responsibility on a passage are as important on a boat at sea as the safety gear aboard. The *Apollonia* gives us a horrifying picture of what happens when this does not go according to plan.

The story of a double murder at sea

Paul Termann, seated in the dock of the Bremen District Court, was a man in his forties, well built, tall and bearded: the stereotypical mariner. Thirty-eight-year-old Dorothea Permin, the woman sitting next to him, was slight of build, and pretty in an insipid way. Neither of the accused seemed to fit the tale of horror the prosecutor was unfolding: double murder and attempted murder on the yacht *Apollonia* during an Atlantic crossing.

The public prosecutor attached to the German port of Bremen had reached a point in the indictment that he wanted to stress: 'None of the persons on board the yacht,' he read out, 'had had sufficient seagoing experience. They were familiar neither with the specific perils of ocean cruising nor with the tensions that, experience has shown, arise out of living at close quarters for lengthy periods. The crew consisted of three groups of two persons each, groups that, up to a few days before departure, were unknown to each other.'

Violence at sea, though as old as seafaring itself, rarely comes before the criminal courts. On the occasions when it has, the acts that have come under inquiry have usually been acts committed by professional seamen. Yet the case before the court now concerned a well-known charter yacht. Not surprisingly, the case shocked many. Commenting on this, Alexander Rost, publisher of the German magazine *Boote*, wrote in the newspaper *Die Zeit*: 'Hardly anyone, moving from an ordered day-to-day existence on land to what is imagined to be an unfettered life of adventure, gives a thought to how quickly, on the wide and open ocean, the ship, the boat, the cabin, can take on the shape of a narrow prison. The seaman has always known this. Hence the precise distribution of duties on board, the strict hierarchy.'

The background of Herbert Klein

Herbert Klein, the owner of the *Apollonia*, was a shipping and forwarding agent from a town near Düsseldorf. He had prospered in the booming German economy and, with his girlfriend, Gabriele Humpert, was in search of wider horizons. In his early thirties, still married but separated, he wanted to take time out in the seductive and, he believed, lucrative world of Caribbean charter.

Klein had bought the *Apollonia* in 1981. She was a long-keeled, 18-ton, 54-foot yawl carrying 191 square yards of sail. In north German cruising circles she was a well-known boat, former flagship of the Segelkameradschaft Das Wappen von Bremen, a pre-war association dedicated to ocean cruising. As the *Wappen von Bremen II*, her previous name, the yacht had logged nearly 300,000 sea miles, completed 24 Atlantic crossings and, in the summer of 1976, became the first yacht to round Spitzbergen at 81° N. Yet the cost of her upkeep forced her sale by the association. In marketing her, the association's magazine portrayed a yacht of no great turn of speed, but with sea-keeping qualities that were quite superb. Klein paid DM180,000 for *Wappen von Bremen II*, and spent a further DM100,000 on refitting her. Contacting a Munich charter agency about his Caribbean plans, he was told to get the boat across the Atlantic as soon as possible.

Klein first met Paul Termann on the quayside at Pasito Blanco, a harbour in Gran Canaria. They seemed fated to meet – Termann was without a boat; Klein was without a crew. The precise reason for Klein's original crew deserting

Apollonia has never emerged. Klein's wife, who had kept in regular contact with him, spoke at the trial of him complaining that his crew had been careless with the boat and that his nerves were at breaking point. She described her husband generally as outward looking, liberal and with a zest for life. Yet according to the original crew, Klein had been sensitive to criticism, aggressive and intolerant. Wherever the actual truth lay, it was out of a mutual predicament that a rapport between Klein and Termann arose and which, in the initial shore-based days, developed into something like a friendship.

Paul Termann's background

Paul Termann was brought up in the Democratic Republic of Germany, and had fled to the West in 1957, hoping for prosperity that never came. Called up in 1960, he signed on for five years in the German army and served as a helicopter cargo pilot. Termann's five years in the army passed without incident, but his file, in a final appraisal, refers to moods that impaired performance, a tendency to pose, and a barely average capacity to cope with stress. He was never promoted to officer rank. After the army, a trip to South Africa followed, where his pilot certificates were not recognised, a fact he could have established in Germany. By 1971 Termann was employed as a long distance locomotive driver with the German railways, and then finally as a driver on the Hamburg Underground – a definite social and professional decline that was not lost on him.

In the 1970s he had become increasingly preoccupied with the sea and sailing and, happening to read of the exploits of a Captain Lohse, signed on for the next round the world voyage in Lohse's yacht *Orion*. For this, Termann and his partner Dorothea Permin paid DM7,500 each. The start was planned for early1981, but Lohse, unable to sell his Hamburg flat, hung on. Termann and Permin, without jobs, lived on board *Orion* for six months. Finally, although the flat was still not sold, *Orion* sailed. But relations between Lohse and the crew became strained, and at the end of August *Orion* tied up in Pasito Blanco. Lohse's financial problems were unsolved, so he flew back to Germany, to reappear in October with fresh plans and a new crew. Termann and Permin were summarily thrown off the boat.

Klein and Termann team up

At the beginning of November, Klein had agreed that Termann and Dorothea Permin would act as crew on the *Apollonia*'s journey to the Caribbean – with Termann as navigator – and that after the voyage Termann would receive a document acknowledging his work on board. After his setback in South

Apollonia, *a traditional long-keeled yawl, racing in the North Sea.* PHOTO: *Helmut Schröder*

Africa, this was of the greatest importance to Termann; it was crucial if he was to find work chartering boats or at a sailing school.

Klein then returned to Germany and came back with two men, recruited by advertisement, to make up the crew: Michael Wunsch, aged 26, newly graduated from business school and in search of relaxation, and Dieter Giesen, 30, landlord of a pub in Constance, who had an urge to see more of the world. Of the two, only Wunsch, who also came from Constance, had experience of sailing, on lake boats – experience enough, in Klein's eyes, to appoint him helmsman.

Apollonia attracted little attention as, towards the end of November 1981, she moved steadily away from the Playa Puerto Rico towards the open sea: she was a conventional yacht embarking on a conventional run. However, on board *Apollonia* little was conventional: neither the crew's total sum of experience, nor their conflicting attitudes towards the voyage. To Klein and his girlfriend, Gabriele, it was an adventure; to Wunsch and Giesen, a holiday; to Termann and Dorothea, a bitterly earnest matter.

This aspect of Termann's character, undetected on land, dominated life on board in the coming days. Through years of evening classes, Termann had acquired a theoretical knowledge of seamanship infinitely superior to Klein's. What Termann said was mostly sound, but uttered in such a schoolmasterly tone, a know-all manner, that the crew found it impossible to accept. In particular, Termann criticised everything to do with safety, from the absence of man-overboard manoeuvres and allocation of duties in case of emergency, to the location of flares, and the operation of the liferaft.

As the days passed the atmosphere deteriorated steadily. While Termann and Dorothea's taste in music lay with Elvis Presley, Klein and Gabriele played reggae to excess. On one occasion, during fair weather, Termann discovered a knot that had been improperly tied, woke Klein, and delivered a lecture on safety. Next, a gale, which might have united the crew, had the opposite effect. The yacht rode out the gale with ease, and the crew, led by Klein, registered Termann's continuing strictures with scorn. With Termann to some extent discredited, life on board relaxed. Breakfast was no longer taken together, commands were no longer discussed, and watches were unevenly kept. There was one occasion when Klein rigged a 60-foot warp to the stern of the yacht, tied himself to an end, and lowered himself into the sea to be hauled, howling with glee, through the Atlantic swell. Termann declined Klein's invitation to follow and the word 'coward' was uttered, a word that was to be repeated in different circumstances.

Mounting tensions

The halfway stage was reached and celebrated with champagne, an event to which Termann and Dorothea were not invited. Termann became increasingly resentful and, at the same time, his hatred of Klein grew. As for Klein, each passing mile brought him closer and closer to the Caribbean, to the tough, competitive world of charter with, as he must have seen with increasing clarity, an ageing boat and inadequate sailing experience.

By 13 December *Apollonia* had 500 miles to go and was four days out from Bridgetown. Gabriele made breakfast, but not for Termann and Dorothea. Termann complained and Klein exploded: 'You can make your own breakfast yourself in future. At the next port you are getting out, anyway.' At midday, at the end of his watch, Termann went below, then called Klein into the cabin. Pulling out a revolver, Termann ordered Klein to sign four blank sheets of paper and informed him that he was taking over command of the ship. The first reaction of the ship's crew was total disbelief. Termann then ordered Klein and Gabriele to smoke a last cigarette. 'You're a coward,

Herbert, aren't you?' Termann said, according to the evidence of Michael Wunsch. 'Yes,' replied Klein, 'I am.' This pleased Termann, who ordered scrambled eggs to be served. As the crew ate, Termann repeatedly threatened that Klein and Gabriele would not outlive the day, and that with *Apollonia* he was going to hunt down the master of the *Orion*.

The murders

Throughout the afternoon Klein and Gabriele pleaded for their lives, begging to be set adrift in the liferaft. Towards evening, Termann ordered a sail change and, still carrying the revolver, went below to the chart table. The evidence of experts at the trial was that this order did not necessarily mean that Termann was planning to sail shorthanded, but to Klein the order meant nothing else. Returning to the cockpit after helping Wunsch and Giesen with the sails, Klein picked up a pump handle, went below to the chart table, and hit Termann four times over the head. With blood running down his face, Termann seized the revolver and shot wildly out of the cabin, hitting Wunsch in the chest. A second shot, more carefully aimed, fatally struck Gabriele Humpert in the head. Still holding the pump handle, Klein rushed forward and hid.

Night fell quickly. Dorothea Permin, whose comment on the events so far had been: 'Whatever Paul does is right,' picked up a flashlight and went forward with Termann to look for Klein. 'There he is,' cried Permin, spotting Klein in the beam of light. 'Herbert, come and see what has happened to Gabriele,' Termann called out. Klein stepped forward, and Termann fired for the third time. Herbert Klein's body went overboard, into the deep, where it was shortly afterwards joined by the body of Gabriele Humpert.

Arrival at Bridgetown

Four days later, *Apollonia* duly completed the crossing, and tied up in Bridgetown. Wunsch's condition was stable, but he and Giesen were too terrified by Termann's threats to contradict the preposterous story Termann was telling: that during a storm, Gabriele Humpert had drowned, and Klein, wild with grief, had begun shooting wildly a day or two later, hitting Wunsch, then killing himself.

But of course there had been no storm. The police knew this from both the satellite weather photos and a yachtsman who had been in the area. The German consul, a keen sailor, noticed that the log had several pages missing, and that four pages had been written up together. But for as long as Wunsch and Giesen kept quiet, the police were powerless. They padlocked *Apollonia* and, just before Christmas, put Termann, Dorothea and Giesen on a plane to Germany. The injured Wunsch followed a month later. Finally, in the familiar surroundings of Constance, Wunsch and Giesen went to a lawyer.

The trial

The trial in November 1982 turned, it seemed, on the novel thesis put forward by the defence that homicide in mid-ocean, arising out of tensions on board a sailing boat, could not amount to the crime of murder. Much expert psychiatric evidence was called in support of this. But beyond remarking that the victims were also at fault, thus acknowledging aspects of the defence argument, the court ruled that the issue of stress was not the central issue. Termann had truly intended to kill, partly in desperation at one more failure, partly out of a desire for revenge. Paul Termann received 15 years for attempted murder, and a double sentence of life imprisonment. Dorothea Permin, for her role in the murders, was imprisoned for three years.

But why, if the deaths were planned, had Termann permitted matters to come this far, allowed Wunsch and Giesen to live and tell, and so contrived his own conviction? Was it, as Giesen believed, fear of sailing shorthanded? Was it folly, or too simple a trust in the power of threat? Or was Termann, as his defence maintained, overwhelmed by a storm of aggression towards Klein and Gabriele Humpert?

Why did it go so wrong?

This tragedy aboard the *Apollonia* in 1981 aroused considerable publicity and comment. The case grabbed my attention because I was a keen amateur yachtsmen at that time and also, as a psychiatrist, I had assessed many murderers to provide court reports. I was asked about the case both by forensic psychiatrists and by fellow sailors. There are a number of lessons to be learnt from this macabre tragedy.

Fortunately, murder is a very uncommon crime and there is a greater chance of becoming a victim ashore than afloat. If Klein had taken more care in his crew selection he would have rejected Termann as a potential troublemaker; however, it would have been impossible for him to have recognised Termann as a potential murderer. Violence is particularly likely to occur where there is a history of violence, obvious psychiatric disorder, alcoholism or drug abuse. All these warning factors were absent in Termann's case.

Termann was a man whose career had declined, whose self-esteem was vulnerable, and who had unrealistic expectations from sailing and from the voyage. We do not know the inner workings of his mind at the time of the killing or how he achieved such domination over the two young crewmen Wunsch and Giesen – to the extent that they initially backed his story.

Studies of murder show that a terrible killing may often follow quite trivial provocation. The provocation is usually the last straw after a long build-up of tension and anger. This is clearly what happened aboard the *Apollonia*, for it was the argument over breakfast that triggered the fatal outburst. Yet as every reader of detective stories knows, murder requires a murder weapon. The murder weapon in this case was a revolver, and without this weapon Termann, even if homicidal, would have had immense difficulty in overpowering the rest of the crew and carrying out the double killing. Life aboard the *Apollonia* was disordered and acrimonious, and one crew member was deranged and homicidal. This is a nightmare scenario but, even so, had the *Apollonia* not been carrying firearms it is almost certain that she would have reached Barbados four days later with skipper and crew alive. There would then have been a prompt and acrimonious parting of the ways – something that is fairly common when strangers make up the crew of a disorganised boat. This had already happened to Klein at the end of the *Apollonia*'s first and shorter voyage to the Canaries. The advisability of carrying firearms on an ocean-going yacht has been much debated. Some favour firearms on the grounds of protection and safety; however, a firearm in the hands of an intruder or an angry and deranged crew member is far from safe. A firearm may be the means of changing a dangerous and threatening situation into a fatality; this is exactly what happened on the *Apollonia*.

Murder and derangement at sea may be rare, but stresses and rivalries like those aboard the *Apollonia*, although in a milder form, are quite common. Confinement aboard a small yacht on a long voyage often creates immense tensions. Klein committed a number of errors of judgement, all of which contributed to the stresses aboard the *Apollonia*. Hopefully we will never have to face a murderer, but these errors contain lessons for us all.

Inadequate leadership

Klein lacked both the theoretical knowledge and practical experience to command a yacht on a long voyage. In this situation it is foolish to 'strengthen' the crew by taking a partially experienced 'unknown' from the dockside. This is a recipe for split leadership and for rivalry. And to state the obvious, it is imprudent for an inexperienced skipper to undertake a long voyage on a large boat. Most people have the sense to gain prior experience on small boats and to do weekend and holiday sailing. If experience is lacking it is best to take a paid and experienced professional skipper, and give them a clearly defined role. If professional help cannot be afforded, the voyage should be delayed or modified.

In Marigot Bay, St Lucia, Klein was attracted by the glamour of Caribbean charter, but chartering a yacht anywhere requires leadership and organisational skills.

Crew selection

Emotional difficulties are particularly likely to arise if the crew are unselected and incompatible. On the *Apollonia* the crew can be subdivided into three groups: Klein and his girlfriend, Gabriele (the victims); Termann (the murderer) and his girlfriend, Dorothea; and the two young male crew members, Wunsch and Giesen. There is no evidence that either Klein or his crew had made even elementary enquiries about each other. None of the crew should have sailed with Klein on the grounds of his lack of qualifications and experience. He could produce no references, and enquiries of his previous crew would have revealed temperamental weaknesses. Termann's last skipper had summarily put him off the boat – presumably for a good reason. If Klein had only made proper checks, he might well have recognised that Termann was emotionally unstable and/or a troublemaker, even if there was no actual evidence of mental illness.

Clearly it is sensible for a crew to test their compatibility on a short trip before committing themselves to an ocean voyage. It is likely that a short preliminary voyage in the Canaries would have revealed both Klein's inadequacies as a skipper and the potentially dangerous rivalry between him and Termann.

Watch-keeping and routine

Tensions and rivalries easily develop in the confined space of a yacht on an ocean voyage, and these may be exacerbated by physical discomfort and danger. As we have seen, a properly organised routine of watch-keeping and a careful delegation of tasks is important, and the galley is often an area where minor problems can easily develop into major grievances. The crew need opportunities to sit down together, relax, and talk over and defuse any difficulties. Routine on the *Apollonia* was chaotic and broke all these common sense rules. For instance, Klein's exclusion of Termann and Dorothea from the champagne celebration, and then also from breakfast, only increased the couple's sense of isolation and grievance. It is an example of bad leadership and bad decision-making from which no good can come – even though in this case its fatal consequences were unique and unpredictable.

Conclusions (from the tragedy)

There are elements in this bizarre and terrible saga that remain a mystery. The German court did not find Termann to be mentally ill, and we will never know his exact state of mind at the time of the killing. He executed two people in public and took over a vessel, proclaiming that he would use it to 'hunt down' his previous skipper. It would be an understatement to describe him as being both grandiose and deranged. The verdict of a British court might well have been different: his thinking and behaviour were clearly bizarre, and this may well have justified a verdict of manslaughter on the grounds of diminished responsibility. However, the outcome – a long term of imprisonment – would have been the same.

It remains a chilling story for any skipper contemplating taking on strange crew in a foreign port. This tragic outcome was unique, but there are important lessons to be learnt here in avoiding more mundane and commonplace emotional clashes.

The Singlehander

• Ros Hogbin •

In the previous chapter, we considered an extreme case of breakdown in relations between inexperienced skipper and crew, with tragic consequences. This chapter goes on to discuss a particular breed of sailor, answerable only to himself as both skipper and crew: the singlehander. Singlehanders take to the seas by themselves, and their ability to tackle the wind and the waves alone marks them out from other sailors. This 'aloneness', as they face the entire range of sailing conditions, has spurred some singlehanders on to accomplish great sailing feats, and prompted them to record a fascinating range of emotional experiences during their journeys.

Singlehanders are those who have decided to take to the seas by themselves. They are a particular breed, bound together by who they are, what they have sought to achieve, and what they have accomplished. What marks them out from the rest is their ability and desire to tackle the wind and the waves alone. This chapter looks at these personalities, why they sail solo, what it means to do so, and the events that have inspired them.

Why do they do it?

To ask why anyone should want to sail singlehanded is to probe towards the core of their self-fulfilment. Put simply, sailing alone is profoundly satisfying to some people. Being at sea for long periods, where conditions can fluctuate from 'heavenly' to 'diabolical', with plenty of time to think in between, encourages moments of soul-searching and commitment to paper. Seafaring autobiographies can be refreshingly honest in their approach. Often, realisations are unearthed and motivations laid bare as the solo sailor searches for the words needed to convey his or her innermost feelings.

Following the inner voice

Joshua Slocum was the first singlehander to circumnavigate the world. Walter Magnes Teller describes him as 'a solitary venturer listening to the inner voice rather than to the crowd and following it at all cost.'[1] To some extent, this compulsion holds true for all singlehanders and runs as a common thread between them. Vito Dumas, who in 1943 became the first man to circumnavigate south of the three Capes in the Roaring Forties, queried his own reasons: 'Was it to show that all was not lost after all, that dreamers propelled by their inward vision still lived, that romance somehow managed to survive?'[2] Francis Chichester described his circumnavigation as a way of life: 'I am a poor thing, incomplete, unfulfilled without it.'[3]

Bernard Moitessier, with typical introspection, wrote: 'I felt such a need to rediscover the wind of the high sea, nothing else counted at that moment... All *Joshua* and I wanted was to be left alone with ourselves. Any other thing did not exist, had never existed.'[4] For Pete Goss, the realisation that he wanted to race singlehanded around the world was apocalyptic: 'Suddenly I knew what I had been put on this earth for... I felt such conviction that I spoke it out aloud. I wanted it, I knew I could do it, and from that moment on it never left my mind.'[5]

The spirit of adventure

Singlehanders were, and still are, adventure-seekers, shaped by their 'get up and go' attitude. Many were loners in their early years, seeking solace from straitened circumstances and relishing the outdoors and the natural world. Chichester commented: 'I gradually drifted into the habit of setting off on my own into an escape world of excitement and adventure.'[6] Alec Rose used to dream of adventure; Moitessier mentioned the times he spent as a child 'listening to the forest talk'.[4] Robin Knox-Johnston described his bicycle trips as a youngster: 'I always liked to see what's over the horizon... I can't help that. If that's a spirit of adventure, well I've got it.'[7] Goss also tells of an adventurous childhood: 'I've always travelled and travel is adventure in itself... as a kid we used to make boats out of cardboard boxes and go off on imaginary trips.'[8] Chay Blyth talks about adventure as an antidote to modern living: 'We need adventure, Mankind has always needed adventure, and perhaps we need it more than ever in the technological civilisation of the twentieth century.'[9]

The sheer challenge of it

But there is more to it than just adventure. Singlehanding is tough, demanding and not for the faint-hearted. It demands resilience, persistence and sometimes sheer willpower to keep going. Blyth is very clear about how important the 'challenge' element of the singlehanded voyage was to him: 'I simply like to find out how much the human frame can put up with, and to see the sort of effects which are produced both physically and mentally as a result of pro-longed loneliness under trying conditions.'[10] When Mike Golding broke Blyth's record for a non-stop westabout circumnavigation in the mid-1990s, he did not mince words: 'The truth is,' he said, 'I was not seeking solitude, only the record.'[11] He was candid: 'The focus is on the competition... It's not about being out there on my own. If that was all it was, I wouldn't go. I have absolutely zero interest in going sailing on my own.'[12]

For some, the very nature of competitive singlehanding has become so extreme that human endurance is now an overriding consideration. The BOC Challenge is an example of this. Dubbed the longest race on earth for an indi-vidual in any sport, participant Josh Hall sums it up: 'Despite modern technology, the sea is still the same as it has always been – relentless and unforgiving. This will never change and is both the risk and lure for sailors.'[13]

Mountaineers reach for the highest peak 'because it is there' and single-handers cross oceans for the same reason.

The essence of being alone

The world the singlehander inhabits is profoundly different from the world we live in ashore. The singlehander is journeying, never still. The sea may at one moment seem vast and empty, and at another, teeming with sealife. He is close to the elements and his horizon is unbroken. He experiences the freedom and simplicity that life on the ocean wave brings, while being con-stantly aware of the toughness of the voyage. He is in tune with his boat – a bond that may be long lasting. The boat has a unique character; he knows her strengths, faults and foibles. There is no one else around to help with the physical challenges; no one to share the danger when conditions turn nasty. And, on the longer passages, there is the ever-present spectre of exhaustion.

Freedom

'No-one can know the pleasure of sailing free over the great oceans save those who have had the experience,'[1] Slocum commented. This reflection is true, but much can be imagined through vivid descriptions such as Tony Bullimore's account of his first trip out of sight of land: 'I felt exhilarated. There were no roads or one-way signs or traffic lights. I was pushing across a massive move-able canvas; a natural wonder, without which there could be no life on earth.' Neal Petersen, a competitor in the 1994 BOC Challenge, commented, 'I've found a type of freedom you find only in your mind and soul.'[13]

Francis Chichester on board Gipsy Moth IV. *PHOTO: PPL.*

The simple life

In tandem with freedom comes the shedding of complexity. Vito Dumas recognised simplicity as he made his first proper meal in rough conditions: 'Soup and fried potatoes. Not much, but for me a banquet. So one goes on expecting less and less; and any trifle may become a source of satisfaction. Perhaps that is truly living.'[2] In a moment of reflection, Golding touched on a theme common to many sailors: 'The feeling of crossing a wild ocean... completely under your own efforts and not utilising an engine... There are some very pure sides to it, which are very appealing.'[12]

'I live only with the sea and my boat, for the sea and for my boat,'[4] Moitessier claimed. Robin Knox-Johnston added, 'The only reality is my small cabin and the endless empty sea around it... Dealing with the elements in a straightforward manner and with only the basic rules of the sea to go by, things appeared in a far less complicated light than they do when surrounded by the diversions of civilisation.'[14] Tony Bullimore described what he feels once he's covered 1,000 miles: 'That's when the boat and the sea start to grow on me. Slowly I forget about the land and the yacht becomes my world. I feel the heartbeat of the hull beneath my feet.'[15]

One man and his boat

The singlehander is acutely aware of how much he relies on his boat to complete a voyage successfully. At the outset of his circumnavigation through the Roaring Forties, Vito Dumas made this clear: 'For the moment I knew that my safety, my universe, depended on the security of a few planks... The seaman must not think of himself until he has seen to the needs of his craft.'[2] Even 50 years on, this holds true, as Golding wrote: 'In the 1990s, singlehanding has developed to the point that boats are now driven close to their limit 24 hours a day, every day. One needs total confidence in the boat to achieve this.'[11] This belief is crucial, because at any one moment the singlehander is potentially only a hull away from a watery end.

A tough act to follow

The oceans, particularly in the higher latitudes, are not benevolent, and any singlehander choosing to cross them is aware of the hardships he will face. The Southern Ocean has prompted the most vivid descriptions from Blyth and Goss. Blyth wrote: 'The reality was far more horrible than I had imagined. There was a peculiar quality of venom in the seas, a viciousness'[9], and Goss said: 'It's just the magnitude of it... it's like wilderness – fabulous.'[8] A typical circumnavigation may involve extreme conditions for 80 per cent of the time, as Bullimore relates: 'If you choose to go off to sea singlehanded in a little boat... and your boat is smashed to bits... it's not really the sea's fault is it? The fact is, you don't have to be there... The sea won't be kind to you. If it starts to pound big waves at you and it's going to do it all night, it'll do it all night.'[16] Goss adds: 'Never get cocky at sea – it ain't over until the mooring lines have been made fast.'[5] There is no doubt that sailing alone is tough going. As Slocum so eloquently put it: 'To face the elements is, to be sure, no light matter when the sea is in its grandest mood. You must then know the sea, and know that you know it, and not forget that it was made to be sailed over.'

Exhaustion

As well as managing the boat in the widest range of conditions, the singlehander has to establish workable sleep patterns and stave off the inevitable exhaustion that can overcome him at any time. Francis Chichester knew his own limits when he took part in the first singlehanded transatlantic race: 'Last night, from a racing viewpoint, I did an awful thing. I knew I was wasting miles by not setting more sail during the night but I went on strike and turned over under the blankets.'[17] 'What difference does 20 miles make when I have about 20,000 to go?' Knox-Johnston asked, 'I feel altogether mentally and physically exhausted, and I've been in the Southern Ocean only a week.'[14] Mike Golding also commented on his fatigue: 'When I was tired, I found

Mike Golding at the helm of his Open 60 Team Group 4. PHOTO: *Mark Pepper.*

myself working in a trance-like state, moving slowly around the deck in a methodical routine way... my mind often elsewhere.'[11] In the singlehanded transatlantic race, Pete Goss sang to keep going: 'To stay awake, I sang at the top of my voice and I marched around the deck, pausing occasionally to shake my fists skyward and swear at the weather,'[5] and Moitessier waxed lyrical: 'I feel tremendously tired, yet I feel crammed with dynamite, ready to level the whole world and forgive it everything.'[4]

In spite of sleep deprivation, singlehanders must be in touch with the way their bodies and minds work in order to help themselves and make the most of their circumstances. Often they divide their voyages into bite-sized chunks, realising the psychological value of completing one manageable section at a time. They are well aware of the debilitation of injury and the call to self-preservation, as Chichester relates: 'I am not in a hurry; at present I am not going to do a single thing unless I have to. I want to recover from my body blows first and that requires time.'[18] This was echoed by Golding during his quest to better Blyth's westabout record: 'I had become very self-protective and would sooner see a sail flogging or sail in the wrong direction than put myself at risk of further injury.'[11]

Preparing the mind
Singlehanders develop the ability to discipline their minds, adopting 'mind over matter' principles to face hard tasks ahead. Pete Goss always 'practises' for a trip mentally before he sets out: 'I sail the course over and over in my

mind, slowly building up the picture until it is 3-D, in full colour and I can even imagine the smells and noises. I leave nothing out... By the time the start gun goes, I am taking on something that I feel I already know intimately.'[5]

The success of this visualisation technique was demonstrated clearly during the 1996–7 Vendée Globe singlehanded round the world race, where both Goss and Bullimore faced supreme challenges. Bullimore capsized in the Southern Ocean and spent days trapped inside the partially flooded, upturned hull of *Exide Challenger*. In his book *Saved*, Bullimore described his general approach to problems: 'By my nature, I spend a lot of time thinking before putting a plan into action... [to] think things through the whole way and to look at every possibility and contingency.' As he faced this battle for his life, he thought through scenes that might help him find the strength he needed to stay alive. In this same race, Goss was cast as rescuer, rather than victim, when he received the call that Raphael Dinelli had capsized 160 miles upwind of him in hurricane-force conditions. Goss turned and beat his way back to save him: '[I] mentally walked the course a few times... Every visualised run culminated in a successful rescue.'[5]

Extremes of emotional experience

Besides exercising the mind cerebrally, all seafarers, and perhaps single-handers in particular, find that their emotional parameters shift considerably while they are on passage. They leave the behavioural norms dictated by land-based society, and are suddenly confronted with the possibilities of pushing emotional boundaries to their very limits and 'letting rip' with their feelings.

Emotional hothouse

'For me the race was a mixture of frustration, fear, calm reflection, and intense elation. The thing that distinguishes long-distance passage-making alone from almost any other undertaking is its capacity to deliver such extremes in emotional experience,'[19] commented Nigel Rowe, as he described his participation in the 1994–5 BOC Challenge. Moitessier spoke of extended time at sea: 'I never thought it possible to attain such fullness of body and mind after five months in a closed system,'[4] and Chichester continues the theme: 'My sensations were all greater; excitement, fear, pleasure, achievement, all seemed sharper.'[20] Goss described the concentrating effect of the non-stop Vendée Globe challenge: 'It was like four and a half years of life condensed into four and a half months. The highs are very heady and the lows were quite crushing.'[8]

There is no doubt that singlehanders experience a whole range of emotions in a much stronger way at sea. Mood swings and extremes of behaviour are frequently catalogued in journals and published works, sometimes with an accompanying note of surprise. Rowe's comment when he found himself becalmed is typical: 'I stood in the cockpit panting and screaming before collapsing into a corner, crying and laughing. Much more of this and I would go mad, I thought.'[19] Periods of joy take their place alongside loneliness, frustration and fear in the singlehander's emotional inventory.

On the bright side

To his critics, Chichester was 'mad' to go in for the first singlehanded transatlantic race, yet Chichester himself wrote: 'What do I care, I haven't enjoyed myself so much for years.'[17] In Blyth's punishing 'impossible voyage', circumnavigating against the prevailing winds and currents, he recounted moments of pleasure: 'Today I feel utterly contented with my lot in life. Few times do I ever feel it, but today was one of them. It's a very pleasant feeling, sheer bliss.'[10] Tony Bullimore also recalls enjoyable times in an otherwise challenge-centred lifestyle: 'It's one of those rare days when everything comes together and you feel a remarkable affinity with the boat and your surroundings... I sit at the helm and glory at the silence and the sheer sense of space.'[15] Goss adds: 'What is more fantastic than to stand at the bow of a boat that you helped bring to fruition as it surges along?... I feel so alive when I am out there with an unblemished horizon and the musical rush of water passing the hull.'[5]

Loneliness

Many singlehanders are naturally loners, who are at ease in their own company and function well by themselves. Some feel the isolation keenly from time to time. Slocum found that keeping busy during the rigours of a gale occupied him enough to prevent him dwelling on his lonely state. Others are not as susceptible to the despair of true loneliness.

Chichester found that being alone in the Atlantic was like a 'warm friendly party' compared with the loneliness he felt in his early land-based years in New Zealand, and Alec Rose commented on the difference between being 'alone' and 'lonely', suggesting that big cities can be much lonelier than the oceans. Knox-Johnston, although jolted by feelings of loneliness at the start of his non-stop circumnavigation, divides singlehanded racers into two types: 'There aren't many natural singlehanders. A lot of people do it, because they think they ought, but there are not many, like me, who are quite happy on their own. I'm very happy on my own. It doesn't mean I don't like company, I do, but I can get in a boat and sail singlehanded and be very competitive at it, whereas an awful lot who do it are not really competitive, their performance drops, because they need someone else there to stimulate them.'[7]

Anger and frustration

'It isn't rational,' Chichester noted, when becalmed during his transatlantic race, 'here I am biting my mental fingernails through frustration and yet if I arrived and returned to a city life I should be thinking of such a jaunt as this all the time and wishing I were away on it.'[17] He spoke for many singlehanders who wrestle with the dichotomy between 'civilised' life ashore and the pent-up aggravation that besets them on a long voyage, particularly when they are unable to make progress. Nigel Rowe describes vividly the destructive effects of being becalmed: 'That afternoon I stood in the cockpit, clenched fists in the air, and screamed at the top of my voice "GIIIIIIVE MEEEEE MOOOOOOORE WIIIIIIND!" I stamped my feet. I thumped the dodger with my fist till it hurt. Then I did it all over again.'[19] Knox-Johnston was realistic about how he felt: 'It is just as well that I am on my own... I am not the sort of person that takes adverse conditions calmly and my mood at present is murderous.'[14]

Fear

One of the strongest emotions faced by the majority of singlehanders is fear. This is particularly well documented by racers and those undertaking severely testing voyages. The Southern Ocean and Cape Horn in particular have struck fear into the hearts of yachtsmen for generations. 'The frightening reality of what lay before me, was to surpass anything I had experienced before in my life as a sailor,'[2] Dumas foretold as he headed back down into the Roaring Forties. Blyth described being 'honestly and genuinely frightened', for the first time in his life, when he was faced with a storm near Cape Horn. Some racers see the experiencing of fear as a part of the 'package' they take on when they agree to sign up. Nigel Rowe found he was beset by emotional numbness for part of his BOC Challenge attempt and was relieved when his feelings returned: 'At last the nerve-endings of my feelings and emotions were coming back to life... Strangely I found this a welcome development. It would have been dreadful to have come all this way and not experience true raw fear!' Josh Hall summed up his reason for participating in the same race: 'I'm out there to scare the living daylights out of myself... I believe we're all addicted to living on the edge sometimes.'[13]

'Living on the edge' may provide the adrenaline rush many sportsmen seek to thrill them into even greater competitive endeavour, however a surfeit of adrenaline was nearly Mike Garside's downfall as he headed for the start of the 1998–9 Around Alone race. With characteristic drive and focus he had prepared his new boat, and set sail alone across the Atlantic. He found his first experience sailing solo out of sight of land so frightening that he 'turned on an adrenaline tap'. 'Everyone has a natural level of fear,' he commented. 'As you get older, you get more fearful. It's just a fact of life...

I tried to analyse it at the time – why am I so frightened? You can only die: I don't want to die!' Back in England, continuous excess adrenaline made him feel permanently sick. He tried beta-blockers: 'That helped enormously but I felt it's absolutely wrong to be taking a drug to cure a problem which goes right to the soul of a person.' As a shot in the dark, he consulted a hypnotherapist and learnt self-hypnosis. 'It's a question of relaxation. If you're not fit physically, you have to go and do weight training and running. If you're not fit mentally, you have to find ways of getting fit mentally.'[21] Garside conquered the debilitating effects of his fear and went on to complete a successful Around Alone race.

Mike Garside at the end of the 1998–9 Around Alone race. PHOTO: Mike Garside.

At a deeper level

Think, think, think

With an abundance of time to think, singlehanders can sometimes become introspective, examining and re-ordering their priorities and values. Although Moitessier was ahead of Knox-Johnston in the Golden Globe non-stop circumnavigation challenge, he decided that the pressures of completing a round the world race were not for him: 'Round the world goes further than the ends of the earth, as far as life itself, perhaps further still. When you sense that, your head begins to swim, you are a little afraid.'[4] To be true to himself, Moitessier forfeited the possibility of winning the race and continued on past the Cape of Good Hope for the second time, ending up on the South Pacific island of Tahiti.

In contrast, Mike Golding preferred *not* to spend too much time thinking inwardly. He converted this energy into a quest for greater boat speed, avoiding the 'reefs of soul-searching'.[11] 'The more I've got involved,' he says, 'the more I've started to become fascinated by the chess-like aspects of sailing – the psychologies of the different players.'[12] When Bullimore had to face the prospect of approaching death, he made an agreement with himself *not* to think about dying for another day. Rowe also tells of a 'subconscious protective mechanism' in his mind that numbed his emotions and helped him to deal with a Southern Ocean passage: 'My emotional passage through this potentially treacherous ocean had delivered my mind to a curious state. It felt as if my feelings were cushioned from any excesses, good or bad. That part of my mind that could sense extremes of excitement or fear had been closed down.'[19]

Is there anyone out there?

The ability to think beyond the purely material is common to many single-handers. Chichester commented on the Roaring Forties: 'Another thing which I find hard to describe, even to put into words at all, was the spiritual loneliness of this empty quarter of the world... the North Atlantic seems to have a spiritual atmosphere as if teeming with the spirits of the men who sailed and died there. Down here in the Southern Ocean it was a great void.'[3] Knox-Johnston wrote with great honesty about his own views on things spiritual: 'When everything has been done that you know you can do, you put your trust in your Superior Being... there is a great deal of comfort to be gained by thinking that there is something out there that can protect you. Because of this belief, throughout the voyage I never really felt I was completely alone, and I think a man would have to be inhumanly confident and self-reliant if he were to make this sort of voyage without faith in God.'[14]

During his westabout circumnavigation, Blyth sought refuge in prayer, which seemed to bring his family closer and refresh him. In tough times he commented: 'No one will ever say to me that there is no God without my remembering all these situations. To atheists I say, "Go sailing singlehanded for a few weeks." '[9] In today's world, where a spiritual starting point may be non-existent, seafarers still have cause to wonder at the huge power and grandeur of the natural elements. Pete Goss's view is a practical one: 'I don't go to church, I wouldn't know how to pray and if the boat was sinking, the last thing I'd do is get on my knees and pray. I'd get a bucket and bail.'[8] But still Goss considers it very important that all his boats are blessed.

Keeping in touch

Communications

Up until the 1960s, on-board communications were very rare and attitudes towards them were correspondingly negative. Early singlehanders had to be utterly self-sufficient. Blondie Hasler's rules, set out in 1957 for the first sin-glehanded transatlantic race: The Observer single-handed trans-Atlantic race (OSTAR) which took place in 1960, stated that: 'No form of radio transmitter may be carried. This is to prevent yachts from calling for help or reporting their position, except when within range of visual or sound signals.'[22] Chichester did carry a radio telephone, but was put out by the demands of it. 'The radio mars the serenity of an adventure like this,'[17] he said. He felt under pressure to deliver newsworthy material: 'I am beginning to dread transmitting nights, and I fear losing my enthusiasm for worthwhile dispatches.'[3] He wanted to round Cape Horn without any intrusions after 50 days' solitude in the Southern Ocean. One reporter asked him what he had eaten first after rounding the Horn, to which he retorted '[I] strongly urge you to stop questioning and interviewing me, which poisons the romantic attractions of this voyage!'[3]

Those left behind

A further reason why many singlehanders detested early on-board communications was the accompanying pressure of contacting their supporters and loved ones ashore. Alec Rose took a transmitter round the world with him, but he was still concerned about propagation failure: 'I have always been against having a radio transmitter, on the grounds that if no contact was made people ashore would worry.'[23] Moitessier battled with these feelings: 'It is a hard card to play, this need I feel to reassure family and friends... Logic shouts at me to play the game alone, without burdening myself with the others... But for many days another voice had been insisting "You are alone, yet not alone. The others need you, and you need them. Without them, you would not get anywhere, and nothing would be true."'[4]

Knox-Johnston agreed that the demands of modern communications could be a real burden and a distraction to the singlehander. 'One of the great things for me,' he said, describing his circumnavigation, 'was that my radio packed up after about two months. Wonderful! Didn't have to worry about it!'[7] Pete Goss sees the benefits and the drawbacks of modern communications: 'They're brilliant, but sometimes you can have too much communication – you do have to manage it when you're singlehanded, because if you're not careful, you have so much contact that you don't get the opportunity to actually make that final break and to become a singlehanded sailor – it can trap you in the no-man's land in between the two.'[8]

Selfishness

Today, singlehanded racing has taken its place among the full range of professional sporting pursuits, and many lone cruisers pursue their sailing dreams. Early singlehanders, however, were experimenting and exploring their inner need to sail alone and they sometimes lacked confidence in the validity of what they were doing. Knox-Johnston described an 'element of selfishness' in his own trip and the fact that it was 'not advancing science in any way'.[14] Blyth also felt 'dreadfully selfish', as he commented on the degree of focus he required to prepare for his circumnavigation. After completing the voyage he added: 'Yes, I think I must say that this was selfish', but coun-teracted this by adding, 'If life is to mean anything at all, a man must try to fulfil himself.'[9] J R L Anderson, in his introduction to *The Lonely Sea and the Sky*, felt strongly that Chichester was *not* in fact selfish, commenting that, 'he has undertaken whatever project he has set himself with no particular thought of gain, with no demands on others, and with a deep humility of conviction'. He added that Chichester's service to all of us was his 'demon-stration of man's continuing ability to fend for himself'.

After the event

Have you lost your mind?

The pioneer singlehanders of the 1960s aroused great curiosity in shore-based observers, who were eager to find out whether they had been changed by the experience. After his solo voyage across the Atlantic, Chichester was met by a captain of the US Air Force, who wanted to know if he had had any uncanny experiences, or felt peculiar, or if he had done anything odd during his 40 days of solitude. Chichester's own impression, after spending 90 days alone on his way to Australia, was merely that he was 'exuberant with friend-liness, affable and anxious to please'.[3]

The *Sunday Mirror* psychiatrist pronounced Knox-Johnston 'distressingly normal'.[14] Knox-Johnston felt that his reasoning had sharpened and that he would now think more deeply before coming to a decision. Mike Golding confessed that he didn't feel different at all, as he approached the UK on his way to breaking Blyth's record for a westabout circumnavigation.

A matter of opinion

Negative opinions are often much more quickly formed than positive ones and the original idea for the singlehanded transatlantic race was no excep-tion. It provoked a horrified reaction from various quarters, with cries of 'dangerous' and 'hair-brained'. Newspaper correspondence, written after Chichester had completed the first half of his circumnavigation, was deeply sceptical about the ability of self steering gear to withstand the rigours of Cape Horn, and the ability of a singlehander to pay constant attention to the running of the boat. One article commented that 'with such a monstrously small yacht' Francis Chichester was 'asking a little too much of God'.[6]

Such opinions notwithstanding, perceptions have changed and single-handers are a thriving breed. Large yachts are now built specifically to be raced singlehanded. The Around Alone and Vendée Globe challenges have been set up to test the skills of the singlehander to the limit. Issues such as the capsizes, dismastings and casualties that took place in the 1996–7

Vendée Globe, have provoked strong arguments about the tightening up of regulations and alternative views that this would destroy the 'spirit of adventure' inherent in such an extreme sailing events. Authorities such as the RYA have moved on in their thinking. Their new Solo initiative states that they are 'now actively supporting and encouraging single and short-handed sailing... taking a more earnest interest in what previously was seen as a "maverick" form of sailing'.[24]

'Where, after all, would be the poetry of the sea were there no wild waves?'[1] Joshua Slocum said more than 100 years ago. Singlehanders continue to tackle this wilderness alone, with adventurous spirits, trusty boats and sturdy hearts. Long may they succeed!

REFERENCES

[1] *Sailing Alone Around the World*, Joshua Slocum, Penguin, New York, 1999.

[2] *Alone Through the Roaring Forties*, Vito Dumas, Adlard Coles, London, 1960 and International Marine, Camden, Maine, 2001.

[3] *Gipsy Moth Circles the World*, Francis Chichester, Hodder & Stoughton, London, 1967 and International Marine, Camden, Maine, 2000.

[4] *The Long Way*, Bernard Moitessier, Granada, London, 1974 and Sheridan House, Dobbs Ferry, New York, 1995.

[5] *Close to the Wind*, Pete Goss, Headline Book Publishing, London, 1998 and Carroll & Graf, New York, 1999.

[6] *Francis Chichester*, Anita Leslie, Hutchinson, London, 1975 and Walker, New York, 1975.

[7] Sir Robin Knox-Johnston interview, January 2000.

[8] Pete Goss interview, February 2000.

[9] *The Impossible Voyage*, Chay Blyth, Hodder & Stoughton, London, 1971 and Putnam, New York 1972.

[10] *Innocent Aboard*, Chay Blyth, Nautical, London, 1970.

[11] *No Law, No God*, Mike Golding, Hodder & Stoughton, London, 1994.

[12] Mike Golding interview, January 2000.

[13] *The Loneliest Race*, Paul Gelder, Adlard Coles Nautical, 1995.

[14] *A World of My Own: The Single-handed Non-stop Circumnavigation of the World in Suhaili*, Robin Knox-Johnston, Cassell, London, 1969 and Morrow, New York, 1970.

[15] *Saved,* Tony Bullimore, Little, Brown & Co, London, 1997.

[16] Tony Bullimore interview, January 2000.

[17] *Alone Across the Atlantic*, Francis Chichester, Allen and Unwin Ltd, London, 1961 and Doubleday, Garden City, New York, 1961.

[18] *The Romantic Challenge*, Francis Chichester, Cassell, 1971 and Coward, McCann & Geoghegan 1972.

[19] *Around the Big Blue Marble*, Nigel Rowe, Aurum Press Ltd, London, 1995.

[20] *The Lonely Sea and the Sky*, Francis Chichester, Hodder & Stoughton, London, 1964 and Coward-McCann, New York, 1964.

[21] Mike Garside interview, January 2000.

[22] *Blondie*, Ewen Southby-Tailyour, Leo Cooper, Yorkshire, 1998.

[23] *My Lively Lady*, Sir Alec Rose, Nautical Publishing Company, London, 1968 and D McKay, New York, 1969.

[24] RYA Solo website www.ryasolo.org.uk

The Last Voyage and Death of Donald Crowhurst: a Reassessment

• Peter Noble •

There are few more fascinating nautical stories than that of the singlehander Donald Crowhurst. At 7.50 am on 10 July 1969 at latitude 33° 11' north and longitude 40° 28' west, the Royal Mail vessel *Picardy* sighted a small trimaran ghosting at 2 knots under mizzen sail on the calm Sargasso Sea, part of the North Atlantic Ocean. Hailing produced no response, the *Picardy* stopped to investigate. The trimaran, which was unattended, was Donald Crowhurst's *Teignmouth Electron*. Crowhurst had sailed from Teignmouth on the previous 31 October to compete in the Golden Globe singlehanded round the world race. Messages from him had indicated that he had survived the Roaring Forties and Cape Horn and was now leading the race home. It was thus popularly believed that, but for his loss at sea, success, fame and fortune would have awaited him in England.

Captain Richard Box winched the empty trimaran aboard the *Picardy*. Subsequent examination of Crowhurst's logbooks, diaries and tape recordings by the journalists Nicholas Tomalin and Ron Hall[1] revealed an intriguing mystery of the sea: the story of one man and how the failure of an ill-prepared voyage led to deception and fraud, and finally madness and death.

The Golden Globe Challenge

The earlier achievements of solo circumnavigators such as Francis Chichester had led to the idea of a singlehanded round the world race to be known as the Golden Globe Challenge; and in 1968 *The Sunday Times* sponsored the first race with a prize of £5,000 for the fastest time. Nine competitors started from Europe between the deadlines of 1 June and 31 October. However, most of these competitors sustained damage to their boats and retired from the race.

The celebrated French solo yachtsmen Bernard Moitessier, in his rugged boat

Joshua, rounded Cape Horn well ahead of the field. However, in a mystic and exultant frame of mind he then abandoned the race to continue in the Roaring Forties, rounded the Cape of Good Hope for a second time, and returned to the Pacific island of Tahiti. Moitessier believed that he had achieved 'union with nature' – his wife took the more prosaic view that his mind had been unhinged by months of solitude. The eventual winner of the race, and in fact the only competitor to complete it, was Robin Knox-Johnston, a tough, young, ex-merchant marine officer sailing the tiny but strong wooden ketch *Suhaili*.

Donald Crowhurst was 36 years old, married with four children, and living in Bridgwater in Somerset. Yet behind this respectable façade there were indications of instability. His widowed mother had suffered from a mental disorder that had led to various attempts at suicide and had spent part of her life in psychiatric institutions. As a youth, Crowhurst had been confident, daring and technically brilliant, and had a passion for fast cars. He was commissioned as a flying officer in the RAF, but after various escapades was asked to resign in 1956. He promptly enlisted as an officer in the army, but once again was asked to resign after further exploits – including car crashes, a prosecution for driving while uninsured, and a drunken attempt to steal a car. After a number of short-term employments he set up his own company, manufacturing radio direction finders for yachtsmen.

Crowhurst was ambitious and plausible but he lacked the steadfastness and reliability to achieve success. When he entered the race, his company was in chronic financial difficulty and he believed that the publicity from winning the Golden Globe Challenge would bring commercial success. Over the years, Crowhurst's friends have given accounts of his character. Many said that he was flamboyant and confident, but also unreliable. He tried too hard to impress. One person said, 'Donald was not a man to go into business with...' His sailing experience was limited: he was a keen weekend yachtsman, but he had no experience of ocean sailing.

Crowhurst's preparation for the race

Initially Crowhurst tried, unsuccessfully, to 'borrow' Chichester's *Gipsy Moth IV* for the race, which was then owned by Lord Dulverton. He then made several desperate attempts to raise money before eventually finding some last-minute sponsorship from a local businessman and also from the council of the seaside town of Teignmouth in Devon. Despite this, he was still short of funds so he re-mortgaged his business. As a result of these efforts, he was able to commission *Teignmouth Electron*. By this time, only three months remained to complete building, fitting out, sea trials and provisioning before the race deadline of 31 October. The boat, a modified and strengthened version of the Victress Class of 41-foot trimarans, was named after his municipal sponsor.

Donald Crowhurst at the launching of Teignmouth Electron *on 23 September 1968. 'I am going because I would have no peace if I stayed.'* PHOTO: News International.

The choice of a small trimaran for such an arduous ocean voyage was foolhardy. Trimarans are at risk of capsizing in strong winds and rough seas. The race course lay through the Southern Ocean where mountainous seas and gales are inevitable. To counteract this risk, Crowhurst had invented a series of electronically controlled gadgets, including an inflatable masthead buoyancy bag, which was intended to prevent a 180° capsize. However, none of these 'inventions' was ever properly installed or in working order, and *Teignmouth Electron* left pitifully unprepared for the voyage. Hatch seals were leaking and even the materials for basic repairs were not stowed aboard. Suction tubing for the bilge pumps had been forgotten and thus the pumps did not work. On the plus side, though, there were adequate supplies of water, food, fuel, charts, a radio transmitter and navigational equipment.

The voyage

After leaving Teignmouth on 31 October, Crowhurst made slow progress southwards. This is not surprising: he was an inexperienced sailor, he lacked ocean racing skills, and his boat was badly prepared. On 15 November he recorded in his log a realistic nine-page summing up of his difficulties: leaks had to be bailed by hand, safety apparatus did not work and the self steering gear, vital for a successful race, was disintegrating because of inadequate screw fittings. Crowhurst had no means of repairing the damage that would inevitably occur in the rigours of the Southern Ocean. His mood was depressed and indecisive, and he described himself as being 'racked by the awareness that I must soon decide whether or not I can go on in the face of the actual situation'. His notes indicate that he fully realised that he had little chance of winning the race, and would certainly endanger his life if he proceeded into the Southern Ocean.

By 15 November Crowhurst's slow erratic progress had only taken him level with the coast of Portugal. He repeatedly thought of abandoning the race, but was dissuaded by a reluctance to let down his family and sponsors. Having re-mortgaged his business, he would be bankrupt if he failed. He started to consider a bewildering range of options – including returning to Europe or making for Madeira, the United States or Cape Town. He was clearly in a state of indecision and panic, and his flamboyant and unreliable character would determine the outcome. Yet in radio contact with his sponsors and family he concealed his difficulties: he gave increasingly vague and optimistic messages, and from 6 December onwards he began to misrepresent his progress and even claimed to have made a record daily run.

It was from this point on that he began to keep two 'logs' or accounts of his voyage. It therefore follows that by 6 December he had already decided to embark on an elaborate deception. The 'true' log gives his actual positions and shows that he remained in the South Atlantic. This log was the basis of his navigation. The 'fake' log gives a series of false positions which would make it seem that he had circumnavigated the Southern Ocean and rounded Cape Horn before returning to the Atlantic. His 'fake' and 'true' logs were not 'reunited' until 4 May the following year, when he was able to give his true position as he sailed towards Europe as the apparent race leader. The deception was essentially simple. He was like a long distance runner who, trailing the field, hides, misses a lap, and then re-emerges as the leader. Crowhurst had 'hidden' in the South Atlantic while the other contestants were 'lapping' the Southern Ocean. His true voyage and his fraudulent claims are in their different ways remarkable.

In order to understand Crowhurst's deception it is first necessary to follow the strategy of the circumnavigators. An ocean sailing boat takes not the shortest route, but the route that follows the direction of the prevailing or trade winds. Thus the yachts followed the old 'clipper route', which takes best advantage of the trade winds. The course lies south-westerly towards the South American side of the Atlantic and then turns sharply south-easterly towards the southern tip of Africa. After the Cape of Good Hope, the vessel is driven eastwards in the Roaring Forties of the Southern Ocean until Cape Horn is rounded

Crowhurst aboard Teignmouth Electron *before the start of the race on 31 October 1968. The boat was still in an unprepared muddle: helpers had fouled the halyards and hanked on the foresails in the reverse order.* PHOTO: *News International.*

to re-enter the Atlantic Ocean. The Southern Ocean is stormy and unfrequented, and a vessel in these inhospitable waters is unlikely to be sighted. After Cape Horn the track is again in the South Atlantic and lies north-easterly, past the Falkland Islands, towards the equator and then into European waters.

Yachts in modern ocean races such as the Vendée Globe are highly technical and carry satellite receivers and transmitters which enable an exact position to be monitored continually by the skipper and by the race organisers. This equipment was not available in 1968 – for instance, Moitessier carried no radio at all because he believed it to be a dangerous distraction from the proper business of sailing. Apart from rare chance sightings by passing ships, the organisers of the Golden Globe Challenge had no independent evidence of a yachts' progress, but relied on the contestants' own reports of their estimated positions. The receiving radio station had no means of checking the position of the transmitting yacht, and the failure of generators and transmitters often meant that no information was received for months on end. Crowhurst was a marine engineer who knew of these difficulties, and took advantage of them in planning his deception.

Crowhurst's deception

The deception was simple in theory, but difficult and complicated to carry out. Crowhurst knew that all documentation would be scrutinised on his return, so he needed to fabricate a detailed written and tape-recorded account of a voyage that had not taken place. He needed to falsify sextant calculations. Normally a navigator takes a sextant reading of the angle of the sun above the horizon, records the date and exact time, and then calculates a position using a nautical almanac and tables. Crowhurst reversed the process. He started with an imagined position at a particular date and time and then used the tables to calculate the sextant reading appropriate to that position. He gathered information about conditions along his supposed route from radio weather messages, and thus a false record was elaborately calculated.

The task required intelligence, skill and considerable navigational knowledge. At the end of the trip he planned to destroy the actual record and present the false record as evidence of the circumnavigation. Once he had taken the step of pretending to be in the Southern Ocean he was trapped by his own deception: there was no longer any plausible way of retiring from the race without revealing the fraud. His deception was thus a desperate gamble that was almost certain to fail, and must have increased the psychological stresses acting on him. His claimed progress had already aroused suspicions, notably those of Sir Francis Chichester, and if he had returned to London it is likely that he would have been exposed. The publicity was immense and he knew that he would return as either a national hero or a complete fraud.

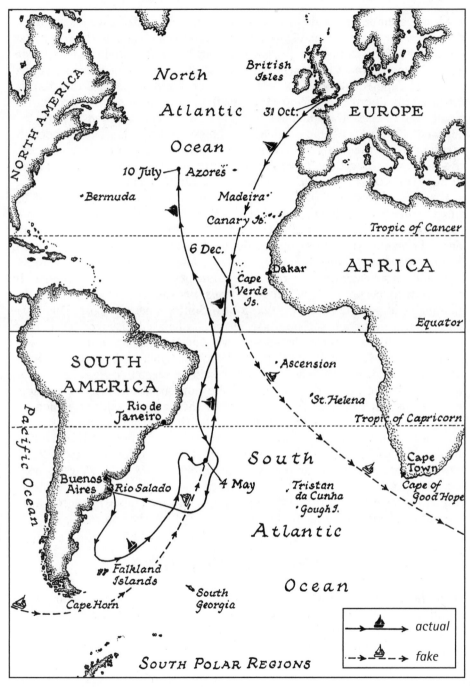

Golden Globe Challenge. Crowhurst's actual route is compared with his fake route.

From December onwards Crowhurst sent back reports of excellent progress as he pretended to circumnavigate the Southern Ocean. The reports were rather vague and always avoided giving his exact position and latitude and longitude. On 24 December, in a Christmas Eve radio telephone call to his wife, he claimed to be 'off Cape Town' when he was in fact on the other side of the Atlantic Ocean within 20 miles of the coast of Brazil. On 19 January he warned that he might need to cease transmissions because of 'generator problems'. There then followed 11 weeks of radio silence – approximately the time needed to circumnavigate the Southern Ocean. On 9 April he sent a radio message that he was approaching Cape Horn, but still gave no exact position. In a further message on 30 April he claimed to be approaching the Falkland Islands.

Yet Crowhurst's 'real' achievements were still remarkable. In spite of his inexperience and an ill-prepared boat he made an actual voyage of over 16,000 miles. (His progress can best be followed by reference to the map.) By March he had spent three months sailing alone back and forth in the South Atlantic well away from shipping routes. This added to his sense of aimlessness and disorientation. By this time, damage and leaks to *Teignmouth Electron* were becoming increasingly serious. Because he lacked the materials for repairs at sea, he decided to stop at a South American port. This must have been a desperate decision, as any landfall risked discovery. Yet in an attempt to maintain secrecy he selected a small Argentinian port, Rio Salado, south of the River Plate. He landed on 6 March, repaired his boat, and departed two days later. One local who helped him said he seemed 'excitable and suspicious', but another said he seemed 'quite normal'. Crowhurst then headed back on his tracks southwards and reached the Falkland Islands, which are clearly shown in a film taken by him at the time; of course, he dared not attempt to land. At one stage he was only 300 miles from Cape Horn, but he then turned back and sailed slowly and irregularly northwards. By radio he learnt of the progress of the other competitors. On 4 May he gave his position as being off the coast of Brazil, which was in fact correct, and placed him as the race leader. On land, the responses to his claimed progress were ecstatic – a hero's welcome undoubtedly awaited him in England.

Mental disintegration

I have reconstructed Crowhurst's mental state from his logbooks, diaries and recorded messages. As we have seen, the deception began in December when he was in a state of pessimism and indecision after realising that he had no chance of winning, or even completing, the race. At that time his mood was depressed but he was still rational and calculating. The deception was carefully planned. For instance, there is evidence that radio messages giving false information were revised many times before being transmitted.

By May, Crowhurst had spent almost six months alone at sea – apart from the two days at Rio Salado. He had endured the pressures of solitude, exhaustion, hardship and danger. The fraud must have added guilt and uncertainty. During May he spent many hours in an unsuccessful attempt to modify his radio in order to set up a radio telephone conversation with his wife. If he had succeeded in speaking to his wife, what would he have told her? Would he have 'played the hero' or would he have 'confessed all'? The impending tragedy might have been averted if he had been able to confess. Instead, in recordings and messages he 'put on a front' and seemed courageous and cheerful; he lied and played the part of the 'returning hero'. Many singlehanders find radio contact with home and family very supportive, but Crowhurst's deception introduced an isolating falsity into all these contacts.

The last navigational entry in his log is a noon sextant position on 23 June. By 24 June, midsummer's day, Crowhurst had become insane. Over the next week, in a burst of frenzied activity, he wrote a longhand journal of over 23,000 words into which he poured his disordered thoughts and preoccupations. The writings consist in part of philosophical speculations on the theme of God, time and eternity. At times the mood is calm or cheerful: 'I feel strangely at peace'. At other times his style is bombastic and exaggerated: some outbursts are totally incoherent. In other passages he is excited and impatient. The text is interspersed with messages in scrawled capitals:

The system IS SHRIEKING OUT THIS MESSAGE AT THE TOP OF ITS VOICE why does no one listen I am listening anyway...

He also shows a grandiose belief in his own scientific abilities and importance:

Mathematicians and engineers used to the techniques of system analysis will skim through my complete work in less than an hour. At the end of that time problems that have beset humanity for thousands of years will have been solved for them. Aspects I have no need to mention will tumble into place, and the distressing struggles of man to reach an understanding of the driving forces between God, Man and the physical universe will be over.

By the third day of the journal he had come to believe that he had solved the secret of the universe:

In just three days the work was done! Christ is amongst us just as surely as if he was walking about signing cheques... I was determined to solve the problem if it took the rest of my life. Half an hour later I had set up the basic equations, and seen the pattern. Three days later I understood everything in nature, in myself, in all religion, in politics, in atheism, agnosticism, communism, and systems. I knew everything from Julius Caesar to Mao Tse Tung. I had a complete set of answers to the most difficult problems now facing mankind.

His revelation of the 'secret of the universe' is interrupted by bombastic outbursts and by puns and jokes. For instance a section is headed 'The Thoughts of Chairman Ja Ac Tarr'. Some comments are incoherent. 'Vengeance of God is mine. Birth Control...'

On June 25 at 5.00 pm *Teignmouth Electron* passed the Norwegian cargo vessel *Cuyahoga*. Crowhurst waved cheerfully and the crew noted that he seemed to be 'in good shape'. He was still able to operate his radio and sent jovial telegrams to his agent. He learned from a radio operator that his wife and family intended to meet him in the Scilly Islands. This seemed to distress him and he tried to dissuade them. Perhaps he had already had intimations of a different rendezvous.

He did not write directly of his fraud but there are foreboding indirect references to sin and concealment. At times his writing is set out like blank verse.

'Nature does not allow
God to Sin any Sins
Except One -
That is the sin of concealment
The Misfit excluded from the system – the freedom to leave the system...
Now is revealed the true
nature and purpose and power
of the game offence...
I am what I am and I
see the nature of my offence
I will only resign this game if you will agree that on
the next occasion that this
game is played it will be played
according to the rules that are devised by
my great god who has
revealed at last to his son
not only the exact nature
of the reason for games but
has also revealed the truth of
the way of the ending of the
next game that
It is finished –
It is finished
IT IS THE MERCY

Crowhurst's preoccupation with time itself increased, and he began to record the time incessantly in his journal. The last entry of 1 July reads:

11 15 00.
It is the end of
my game the truth
has been revealed and it will
be done as my family require me
to do it
11 17 00.
It is the time for your
move to begin
I have no need to prolong the game
It has been a good game that must be ended...
I will play this game
when I choose I will resign the game
11 20 40.
There is no reason for harm.

He writes as if he were talking directly to God and playing out some apocalyptic game with him. The game reaches a climax: 'It is finished. It is the mercy.' Crowhurst no longer has the will to continue playing: 'It has been a good game that must be ended.'

At some point after twenty-past eleven on 1 July Crowhurst stepped from *Teignmouth Electron* in to a calm Sargasso Sea. Nine days later *Teignmouth Electron* was boarded by Captain Richard Bell of the *Picardy*. Crowhurst's life-raft and lifejacket were still aboard, but he had taken with him the ship's clock.

Psychological analysis

What psychiatric or psychological explanations can be given for Crowhurst's motivation and behaviour?

The origins of his deception are to be found in his personality and background. In spite of his many talents, there was a history of fecklessness and unreliability. He was described as 'not a man to go into business with', yet he was plausible and able to talk himself into situations beyond his capacity. As we have seen, he had obtained commissions in both the army and the RAF, but had been sacked on both occasions. He was certainly charismatic, and in obtaining a boat and sponsorship for a round the world race he had again talked himself into a situation that he could not fulfil. He set out on a 'mission impossible' and then gambled on winning by fraud, rather than facing failure and bankruptcy. It is not possible to put forward any psychiatric excuse for this fraud. It was ingenious, elaborate and required the navigational skills that he had learned as a pilot in the RAF. Crowhurst had aspirations for great success, but he lacked the self-discipline and attention to detail required for planning and preparation. This was the root of his problem as a businessman and as a sailor.

In furthering his deception, Crowhurst had spent almost seven months sailing singlehanded, mostly in the isolation of the South Atlantic. As we have already seen in the last chapter, there are many stresses that face the singlehander. Normally, self-belief and a sense of purpose and achievement sustain adventurers and counteract the stresses, but not so for Crowhurst; there was no experience of the 'joy of sailing' to sustain him. He knew that he was a fraud and that he risked failure and exposure, and he was burdened with this extra weight of guilt and foreboding. It is hardly surprising that he was at times anxious and depressed.

By the end of June the potential causes of a serious nervous breakdown were all in place. The diaries indicate a dramatic change in his state of mind, which began sharply on 24 June, a few days before his death. This is the first unequivocal evidence of serious mental illness. His outpourings are typical of a manic illness. Mania is the other side of the coin to severe depression and the two illnesses are linked. Mania is usually precipitated by stress acting on a susceptible individual. The evidence shows that all the characteristic features of mania were present in Crowhurst. These included a sudden onset of over-activity, cheerfulness, excitement, rapid speech or writing, and bombastic self-confidence deteriorating into grandiose delusions. In mania, themes related to the person's circumstances occur in a distorted way and often depression is not far below the surface. Crowhurst wrote 23,000 words in longhand in the course of a week – that is the length of my contribution to this book, and it has taken me many months. He could not have had much time to sleep – and mania is characterised by insomnia and frenetic over-activity.

Brief periods of normal behaviour can occur in mania, and this fits in with Crowhurst's use of the radiotelephone, and his apparent normal appearance on 25 June to a passing ship, *Cuyahoga*. Mania is often precipitated by stress – and the stresses acting on Crowhurst were enormous. There is often a family history of depression: we know that Crowhurst's mother had suffered from psychiatric illness and had attempted suicide. Manic patients often give a history of previous short-lived episodes of overactive and irresponsible behaviour, termed hypomania, and it is quite likely that the 'pranks' for which Crowhurst was dismissed from both the army and the RAF fell into this category.

Consideration must be given to a different diagnosis, but the other possibilities are unlikely. Schizophrenia also causes psychosis, but the hallucinations which are typical of schizophrenia were absent in Crowhurst. Also, the onset of schizophrenia, particularly at the late age of 36, is usually insidious. Starvation and vitamin deficiency have also caused mental breakdowns on long voyages, but again the onset is usually gradual. Crowhurst was thin, but a photograph taken three weeks before his death does not show him to be seriously ill-nourished. He usually had at least one cooked meal a day, and when *Teignmouth Electron* was found there were ample supplies of food aboard. Psychosis can also be caused by contamination of food, medication and poisons, and such organic psychoses are usually associated with confusion and delirium. A bottle of amphetamines containing 32 tablets was found among Crowhurst's medical stores. We do not know whether or not he took amphetamines prior to his breakdown, but amphetamines can precipitate a manic psychosis. Finally, we know that Crowhurst was capable of elaborate fraud. Thus the possibility has to be considered that he was *feigning* mental illness, perhaps with the intention of covering up a suicide attempt. However, the outpourings of Crowhurst's last diary are very similar to the speech and writings of many manic patients that I have treated over the last 30 years and I am certain that they are genuine.

It is clear from Crowhurst's writings that when he stepped from his boat he was deluded and wished to 'resign the game' and in some way fuse 'time and eternity'. He took with him the boat's clock, which suggests that his actions were based on his delusions in relation to time. If he had simply fallen overboard the clock would have been found in the cabin. A belief in supernatural powers is common in mania and may lead to dangerous and self-destructive actions. For example, people may injure or kill themselves in attempts to fly or levitate. Some years ago a patient of mine, a student suffering from mania, deliberately drove a jeep off a 200-foot cliff in order to demonstrate his 'immortality'. Surprisingly, it was a demonstration that was successful – he stepped almost unharmed from the wreckage!

Although chiefly remembered for fraud and for the bizarre circumstances of his death, Crowhurst's genuine achievements as a yachtsman are considerable. He sailed 16,000 miles singlehanded and reached South America, the Falkland Islands, and came within 300 miles of Cape Horn. If he had not been overwhelmed by a serious psychiatric breakdown he would have been capable of sailing the remaining 1,800 miles that separated him from his home port of Teignmouth. Some might even call him a hero, but certainly a tragic hero, destroyed by over-ambition, weaknesses of temperament and finally madness.

REFERENCE

[1] *The Strange Last Voyage of Donald Crowhurst,* Tomalin, N and Hall R, Adlard Coles Nautical, London, 1995 and International Marine, Camden, Maine, 2001.

Communications: Too Much of a Good Thing?

• Ros Hogbin •

In an era in which effective communications and ready access to information are taken for granted, it can be difficult to imagine times past, when the typical sailor severed all links with the shore when he put to sea; when the sum total of weather forecasting rested on personal experience and knowledge of local and seasonal weather patterns. Anyone keen enough to await the arrival of such a yachtsman on some far-off shore would have allowed for substantial margins of error in their estimates. A few short decades later, the way we communicate from ship to shore and between boats has been transformed by technological advancements. It is now almost unheard of for coastal or long distance sailors to set off without at least a VHF radio and a hand-held GPS set, and an increasing number will have at their disposal an array of electronics guaranteed to keep the biggest battery bank hard at work.

This chapter looks at the way in which the communications revolution has altered the way we behave at sea. It explains how the wealth of information available today has certainly inspired confidence, allowing sailors to explore lesser-known islands and anchorages safely. On the other hand, easy access to vast quantities of facts and figures about the sea and the atmosphere can cause us to become complacent, by affecting our perception of risk and perhaps prompting us to make foolhardy decisions. At its worst, we may be in danger of succumbing to information overload as we try to interpret the mass of data arriving on board, and this confusion may in itself have a detrimental effect on the way we sail.

Incommunicado

During his solo voyage through the Roaring Forties in the Second World War, Vito Dumas spent more than 65 days at sea without communications and without speaking to anyone. He could have carried a wireless transmitter on his trip, but he chose not to because of the war; he referred to his experience in the harsh waters of the Southern Ocean as 'a kind of living death'.[1] In the 1960s, yachtsmen were generally still antagonistic towards radio, because it was seen as counter-productive to self-sufficiency and alien to their spirit of sailing. Many went to sea to get away from such intrusions. Some pioneering long distance explorers carried MF transmitters, but used them reluctantly and only out of a sense of duty to sponsors and family.

VHF was introduced in the mid-1960s, but it was not until the 1970s that cruising yachts began to make use of it, even though some cruising yachtsmen at the time, like Mike Garside, were quite content without: 'When we sailed round the world as a family, we didn't have a VHF on board. We had no communications at all. We relied on letters, which we picked up at port offices and that was it. And we didn't miss out.'[2]

The explosion of information technology on land was mirrored in the marine industry, particularly during the 1980s and 1990s, with the introduction of weatherfax and satnav. Most significantly, the advent of GPS revolutionised the way in which sailors obtained their positions and other boat data. As a result, the vast majority of coastal and offshore sailors today travel with some form of on-board communications – ranging from a simple VHF set to the sophistication of a fully interactive satellite system.

Building confidence

Radio
Radio communication has endured for decades, as a low-cost means of transmitting and receiving information. The presence of a radio on board provides a feeling of security, whether it is used inshore to call up the Coastguard, or offshore to confirm the intentions of an approaching vessel. Both VHF and SSB can provide a wide range of weather information via direct broadcasts, Navtex and fax reception. This plays a vital role in yachting safety and may be the primary influence on a skipper's cruising or racing tactics. For the long distance sailor, the SSB still provides some voice and e-mail contact possibilities, although these are rapidly being superseded by satellite options. However, for yachtsmen who wish to keep in touch, whether with family, friends or business associates, it is always thrilling to make contact back to civilisation from a distant anchorage.

SSB radio provides free communication between sailors who are often hundreds, or even thousands, of miles apart. It is still used extensively by ocean cruising yachtsmen. Each season, as a group of cruisers makes its way across the Atlantic or the vast Pacific Ocean, informal 'nets' spring up, through which voyagers on passage can check in with their daily position and weather conditions, and any other information of benefit to those following in their wake. During our circumnavigation, from time to time we

The chart table of Speedwell of Cremyll, *a 49 foot yawl, displaying an array of electronics from the 1960s, 1970s and 1980s. Although this equipment was up-to-the-minute when fitted, it now seems very old-fashioned to the modern eye.* PHOTO: *Tim Bartlett.*

tuned in to a number of different 'nets' and exchanged valuable tips – ranging from which island groups to visit and possible weather changes en route, to the best lure to use when trolling for dorado! When we took part in this, we felt we belonged to an ocean community, albeit a transient one, even though we were in fact isolated from physical contact by thousands of miles of empty ocean. And friendships formed over the airwaves often endured.

Satellites and beyond

'In our increasingly technological world, there is little doubt that the surface hasn't yet been scratched, especially when it comes to electronics,'[3] commented Matthew Sheahan, citing the development of 3-D chart imaging and high speed global internet access. Even without these state-of-the-art refinements, the introduction of GPS has endowed all sailors with the ability to plot their position simply and efficiently and to a high degree of accuracy. Although dead reckoning, position fixing and celestial navigation are naturally still taught in sailing schools, for everyday use GPS has become the standard navigation tool.

The introduction of GPS has inspired great confidence in the sailor. What was once known as a luxury – the ability to plot an accurate position in all

Today's high tech yachts demand state-of-the-art communication systems: the navigation station on board Ellen MacArthur's Open 60 Kingfisher. PHOTO: *Thierry Martinez.*

weathers – has now become commonplace. Knowing precisely where we are has given us boldness in the way we sail. It has opened up access to cruising grounds that were once strictly off-limits to most sailors, such as the Tuamotuan Archipelago in the South Pacific (also known as the Dangerous Archipelago). The Tuamotus are made up of hundreds of tiny low-lying coral atolls, each with an outer reef fringing a shallow lagoon. This lagoon is accessible only via a narrow pass, which must be precisely located and crossed with caution. An accurate GPS position (given to you in advance by a sailor who has already successfully entered the lagoon), accompanied by careful 'eye-ball' navigation, is essential to find the pass, and avoid the hazards surrounding it. You are then sure to be rewarded by wonderful experiences in remote, idyllic anchorages, with all the delights these afford.

Satellite communications have come to the fore in recent years, particularly on racing boats. Coverage is near global and they allow an unparalleled level of sophistication in information management. All racing yachtsmen expect to use them – in sharp contrast to Mike Garside's communications-free cruise of the 1970s, a state that would not have been possible in a modern race. A satellite e-mail facility during the 1998 Around Alone race was vitally important to Garside, as this report shows: 'Early in the race, communications helped to calm the fears and give him confidence, but as he fought to beat J-P Mouligné on the last leg every report spurred him on. "If J-P took a mile off me, I was determined to gain two miles back. Trying to keep going without communications would be very, very difficult." '4 He went on to add, 'I have total respect for the Mini Transat guys who have to go it totally alone.'

Until recently, the Mini Transat, a tough singlehanded race in radical small boats, has been conducted with no communications whatsoever. However, after storm conditions in the 1999 race, prompting a number of avoidable rescues, the organisers considered allowing limited satellite phone use in the case of emergencies. Ellen MacArthur competed in the 1997 race and compared it to the communication requirements that go hand in hand with her sponsored campaigns:

> The Mini Transat's a big test because you really are alone... you can't talk to anybody if you want to. Whereas when you've got the satphone, it's different. Communications are definitely positive when you're on your own. You want to talk to people and make yourself feel better. It's hard to work with the sponsor when you're isolated from them for three and a half months... But it's also for you personally; it gives you an amazing window to share the race through. And it's important for me to share what I'm doing with other people... Because you might be on your own out there but it's everyone who's behind you that helps you.'5

This attitude of responsibility and co-operation with sponsors is prevalent among today's professional racing yachtsmen, who work hard to communicate and share their racing experiences with interested observers.

The BT Global Challenge 2000, involving 12 identical steel boats racing around the world the 'wrong way' with professional skippers and amateur crews, is sponsored by an international telecommunications group, who have provided each yacht with the most comprehensive array of communications equipment: voice-only lines for audio interviews, e-mail and internet access, three separate satellite services, and the capability to transmit digital video footage direct to race headquarters. The on-board communications systems 'will enable crews to share the excitement, tension, physical and emotional demands of the race. Users will also be able to witness how the teams work together to battle the toughest seas in the world... The real opportunity we have with... the internet and the richness of the data coming off the boats is the ability to allow the story to be told from the inside looking out – literally through the eyes, the minds, the hearts of the participants.6

The safety factor

In the early days of ocean racing, Blondie Hasler's view of self-sufficiency was uncompromising: 'No search or rescue operation will be mounted. *Any skipper who is unable to remain alive by his own efforts is expected to die with dignity.*[7] The attitude to safety today is very different. Professionals in major racing events are constantly tracked by race headquarters, who monitor their positions and remain alert for distress calls. The efficiency of this system was put to the test when Isabelle Autissier suffered a catastrophic knockdown to her already jury-rigged boat in the 1994–5 BOC Race: 'slowly the reality dawned as fatigue took over. The steering system was destroyed and she was exhausted from sailing for three weeks with a jury rig in her bid to stay in the race at all costs. "With the state of my boat and my personal state I knew it would not be safe to try and get to Sydney. I had to save what could be saved." ' Two hours after the rollover, and for the first time in her seafaring life, Isabelle took out her distress beacons: 'The small lights began to flash and up there in the stars the satellite picked up my call... When I switched on my EPIRBs I was quite confident of my rescue. I knew it was a good system... It is an incredible organisation.'[8] As a result of the call, search and rescue operations began, co-ordinated by Australia's Maritime Rescue Co-ordination Centre (MRCC) in Canberra, and Autissier's family in France were quickly notified of the emergency situation. A plane arrived 18 hours later. 'When I heard the plane it was a great moment for me. Communication was impossible because my radio was out of action. I sobbed with emotion.' It was almost another 24 hours before she was rescued by helicopter and HMAS *Darwin*, bound for Adelaide. 'I am here because of you and I will never forget that,'[8] she told her rescuers.

Communications provided Tony Bullimore with a life-saving opportunity in the 1996–7 Vendée Globe race. Imprisoned under the hull of *Exide Challenger*, having already activated his distress beacons, he had no idea whether anyone had heard his call. However, the RAAF had responded by mounting the largest peacetime search and rescue operation ever and when Bullimore eventually emerged from the hull, he commented: 'I've been given a second chance at life. From a dark, wet and desperately lonely place, I've been reborn.'[9]

In the same race, while sailing through atrocious conditions in the Southern Ocean, Pete Goss received Mayday relay messages via his satcom system asking him to go to the aid of fellow competitor Raphael Dinelli, 160 miles upwind of him. As he battled against the wind in *Aqua Quorum* to rescue him, Goss spoke to an RAAF rescue plane to ask for position updates. He received detailed weatherfaxes and slowly made his way towards Dinelli's liferaft. In a feat of expert seamanship, Goss successfully rescued the French sailor. On welcoming him aboard *Aqua Quorum*, Goss wrote: 'A feeble "thank you" could be heard from inside the immersion suit... I had no idea that a pair of eyes could convey such a depth of relief and gratitude.'[10] Neither Tony Bullimore nor Raphael Dinelli would have had any chance of being saved without extensive satellite communications systems.

A tendency towards complacency

'In the early days, we didn't have radios, we didn't have EPIRBs, we didn't have all this equipment, we knew we couldn't be rescued. No-one would know where to find us, so you were on your own and it made us much more self-dependent... I think [communications have] made people less self-reliant. This feature of being able to talk to people the whole time is sending people out there who, if their radios broke down, would be lost,'[11] Robin Knox-Johnston commented. This point is valid, particularly with regard to those cruising yachtsmen who seem to use the ability to communicate as an excuse for clogging up VHF channel 16 with a constant stream of radio checks.

In European waters, we are extremely fortunate to be surrounded by safety services: HM Coastguard broadcasts Maritime Safety Information, navigational and meteorological warnings and provides Radio Medical Link Calls on both VHF and MF. Search and rescue operations are co-ordinated by way of GMDSS procedures and consequently many lives are saved around the coast. The airwaves are alive with weather information – from commercial radio stations, on VHF, via SSB weatherfax and satellite systems. We have access to excellent forecasts both for planning purposes and while we sail. We travel with the knowledge that we remain in touch and, should we find ourselves in trouble, professional help is close at hand.

However, this awareness has also, to a certain extent, affected the way we sail. In some cases we rely completely on the forecast we have received, expecting it to be correct in every detail, rather than treating it as a prediction or estimate of forthcoming conditions. We hoist the sails with our minds set on what we have heard and then become irritated if we have to take in a reef or find ourselves wallowing under too little canvas. We blame the weatherman. Worse still, we may hear a forecast signalling bad weather, or advice from the Coastguard about whether to put to sea, and choose to disregard it. Our time may be pressurised: we may have a charter boat to return by a certain deadline. We may think that we can keep ahead of the weather or that the conditions look reasonable enough for us to make a start. In any event, we rationalise, we can always call up the Coastguard if we get into trouble. Our agenda is mixed for our own convenience, often betraying a lack of experience and scant preparation for eventualities. We then expect the rescue services to pick up the pieces. All too often, we hear stories in the press of skippers ignoring advice given by meteorological officers and coastguards to delay departure. They set off under the pressure of deadlines, find themselves in extreme difficulties, and occasionally needless catastrophe results with the loss of crew members overboard.

We have the freedom to choose whether we set sail or not. If we are wise, we will assess the risks and make our judgements accordingly. Inevitably sometimes we will be caught out, as in the 1979 Fastnet Race and the 1998 Sydney to Hobart Race, where the speed, location and depth of the developing depressions caught most people, even forecasters, by surprise. The questions we must therefore ask ourselves are: in the light of the information we have received, will we be sailing within our limits? If the conditions become far more severe than forecast, are we prepared for them? Do we have an effective contingency plan and do we know how to put it into action?

Even differential GPS, giving a geographical position accurate to the nearest few feet, can provide a false sense of security in more remote areas where chart data may be based on surveys from 100 or more years ago. This may render the GPS position inaccurate by as much as a couple of miles when plotted on the chart, which may be of little consequence in the open ocean, but becomes vitally important when locating a narrow pass between coral outcrops in choppy seas. In this situation, we definitely cannot take our GPS position (as plotted on the chart) for granted. For safety we must cross-check visually. It's no use blaming the charts for being inaccurate; some were drawn up when electronics, let alone satellites, were less than a figment in scientists' imaginations.

The plethora of communications on board even the most humble of boats does not mean that we can afford to consider sailing as an exact and precisely controllable science. Indeed, it can be argued that electronics have contributed to the 'de-skilling' of some sailors, and navigators in particular, and so allow 'fools' to put to sea. The richness and variety of the sailing experience exists because of the challenges that the wind and waves afford us. The common sense, ingenuity and skill we use in harnessing air and water to propel us to our destination are part of the joy of sailing, and we adopt a sloppy attitude at our peril. As Pete Goss reminds us: 'Modern equipment and methods do not replace basic seamanship skills, they are simply aids – albeit very good ones.'[10]

Confusion

The *raison d'être* for communications should be clarity – the ability to see a sharper picture, to make a better assessment of a situation, an aid to safe sailing, a means of being in touch. These expectations are not always met. For the early racers, the simple ability to communicate by radio with the shore brought with it unwelcome side effects. Robin Knox-Johnston makes it clear that, when singlehanding: 'The radio schedules are the real trouble, because they don't coincide with your day on the boat, and having to stay up to do the schedule at a set time to suit people ashore is extremely inconvenient, because you should be sleeping or doing something else. If you've got to stop a sail change for a schedule, I think it's wrong. I'd much rather be on satcoms and send my message when convenient.'[11]

Tania Aebi, the 18-year-old singlehanded cruising circumnavigator, who had been out of touch with other yachts at sea for most of her journey, found her sailing 'rhythm' changed when on passage in the company of other boats and within VHF range: 'Instead of developing a natural routine, as on previous passages, my day began to revolve around the radio. I measured time not by the transit of the sun, but by the number of minutes left before I switched on the VHF.'[12]

But beyond these issues of inconvenience, precipitated by slavery to communications, is a much more worrying tendency towards confusion, which can affect any group of yachtsmen at the mercy of information overload.

'Red Sea disorder'

The problems of confusion in the area of communications can be illustrated by one of my own sailing experiences.

When we cruised up the Red Sea in 1999, towards the end of our three-year circumnavigation, we encountered an extreme example of the way in which 'communications overkill' can contribute to an atmosphere of confusion and insecurity. The Red Sea is fascinating both for its variety of cultural attractions and its superb sealife. It is also notorious for challenging sailing conditions and weather patterns, and it was these, in combination with frequent radio communications and a host of human factors (anxiety, seasickness, impatience, changing expectations) that turned a group of easygoing cruisers into frayed, ashen spectres of their former selves.

Specific discussions about the weather – strong headwinds, steep seas and desert dust – began in earnest in Sri Lanka, long before we reached the Red Sea. The majority of that season's yachts destined for the Mediterranean started to tune into the 8 MHz Red Sea net on the SSB each morning, to hear how the boats ahead were doing. We also chatted to boats in our vicinity on 4 MHz as we approached Bab el Mandeb and the start of our Red Sea voyage.

The Red Sea can be divided very roughly into three distinct weather sectors moving northwards: strong southerlies in the first third, a convergence zone with variable conditions midway up, and gale force north-westerlies in the upper third, easing slightly on rare occasions and moderating near Suez. This weather is complicated by the fact that, particularly in the upper third, conditions can change in a matter of minutes from near calms to 25–30 knot headwinds, with very steep seas. In order to allow for this, we all found ourselves waiting in anchorages until the weather seemed clement. We would then set sail at the crack of dawn, knowing that at very short notice and within the space of between 6 and 36 hours the weather would deteriorate, progress would be severely compromised, and the race for shelter would be on. Forecasting these changes was seldom an accurate process, even though an amateur weather watcher in Cyprus broadcast a five-day forecast for the Red Sea three times a week on the SSB.

Our own plans were to cruise up the Red Sea, enjoy the abundant reef life, make what progress we could as conditions dictated, and seek shelter as required. Having reached the port of Suakin in southern Sudan in good time in 20–25 knot south-easterlies, we took advantage of calm convergence conditions to stop overnight at Sanganeb Reef, an area noted for its spectacular diving. This is where we came face to face with the anxieties that changeable weather can bring. Another boat that was anchored nearby cautioned us as they left that afternoon that we were wasting an important weather window by staying overnight while the conditions were calm. Other boats had bypassed the reef altogether and pushed on ahead, anxious to keep moving at all costs. With so much uncertainty in the weather conditions, the 'right' answer about when to move from one anchorage to the next became impossible to assess. As a result, cruising sailors craved ever more information in the hope that this would help them. Radio communications increased sharply, with the supposition that the better informed we were and the more we kept in touch, the easier it would be to find the perfect solution – when in fact there wasn't one.

The radio nets became more urgent. Twice-daily SSB schedules cascaded down from the upper portion of the Red Sea to where we had dropped anchor. Distant, edgy voices spoke of week-long gales, delays and very slow progress. Cruisers further down quizzed the leaders, demanding details of suitable shelter in inhospitable desert inlets. Everyone listened, commented, and made plans over the airwaves. Designated VHF ship-to-ship channels buzzed incessantly. A strange local atmospheric phenomenon meant that VHF traffic could be heard from over 100 miles away, adding to the confusion and disorientating the listener. Eventually, we too were hit with gale-force headwinds and sought shelter in desert inlets; stuck sometimes for a week or more. Not wishing to miss an opportunity, some became impatient and hyper-sensitive to the exact movements and travel plans of others. We crawled our way to windward along the coast. Many lost their independence and succumbed instead to 'herd mentality', travelling in packs and constantly monitoring their anemometers for the first sign of a wind change. While within sight of other boats, some would call one another on the VHF to ask for precise details of their travelling companions' positions, what wind they had at that particular moment, and how soon they would be changing tack.

We had made plans to meet family in Cyprus, and we thought we'd allowed plenty of time to arrive comfortably. As we found our progress hampered, our weekly SSB link call to the United Kingdom became a frustrating experience, as we tried to remain optimistic about reaching Larnaca in time – when in fact gales had allowed us to make good a mere 30 nautical miles in seven days. We tried to stick to our own plans in the face of radio comments that became tainted by a manic edge, as cruisers spent two months battling up the very long 1,200-mile stretch of water. The Red Sea nets aimed to be helpful. However, far from remaining loose-knit and informal, on occasion they took on the characteristics of a military operation, where failure to check in sent a flurry of concern caterpaulting down the fleet. Sometimes the only way to achieve peace and quiet was to turn the radios off.

By the time we had reached the Suez Canal, we were exhausted and relieved to escape the clutches of the Red Sea. Having regained a degree of normality, we listened in to our friends, some still hundreds of miles behind us, stuck as we had been and frustrated by having to listen to well-meaning voices on the radio, voices of experience, passing on masses of information of limited use and leaving the listeners to sift through it and make decisions as best they could. The Red Sea was indeed a fascinating waterway, but demanded substantial psychological preparation to emerge from it in good mental shape.

Communications concluded

In recent history, we have seen on-board communications developing in a major way, alongside yacht design and the challenges we set ourselves on the high seas. The wind and the waves continue to present us with the same pleasures and pitfalls; and we respond with ever more accurate means of positioning ourselves on the oceans, monitoring the weather, and keeping in touch with others. Anyone, if they wish, can still head out to sea in complete simplicity, without so much as a VHF to intrude into their watery world. Most, though, choose to embrace the communications age, recognising in their on-board systems, powerful aids that will add to the enjoyment and competitiveness of their sailing experiences.

Communications options are likely to multiply in the future and enable us to do new things, as boats become faster, races tougher, and our demands to keep in touch greater. Their sophistication will increase, and with it our confidence in them. Conditions at sea today may not differ appreciably to those faced by sailors of yore, but the way we respond to those conditions and manage our sailing is made far more complicated by the amount of data we receive at sea. Ultimately, though, we depend on ourselves to avoid complacency and confusion, use our on-board communications wisely, and practise good seamanship whenever we sail.

REFERENCES

1 *Alone Through the Roaring Forties*, Vito Dumas, Adlard Coles, London, 1960 and International Marine, Camden, Maine, 2001.
2 Mike Garside interview, January 2000.
3 'Leading Edge', Matthew Sheahan, *Yachting World*, January 2000.
4 'Alone with their Thoughts', *High Seas*, September 1999.
5 Ellen MacArthur interview, January 2000.
6 *The BT Global Challenge Review*, May 2000.
7 *Blondie*, Ewen Southby-Tailyour, Leo Cooper, Yorkshire, 1998.
8 *The Loneliest Race*, Paul Gelder, Adlard Coles Nautical, London, 1995.
9 *Saved*, Tony Bullimore, Little, Brown & Co, London, 1997.
10 *Close to the Wind*, Pete Goss, Headline Book Publishing, London, 1998 and Carroll & Graf, New York, 1999.
11 Sir Robin Knox-Johnston interview, January 2000.
12 *Maiden Voyage*, Tania Aebi, with Bernadette Brennan, Hodder & Stoughton, London, 1989 and Simon & Schuster, New York, 1989.

Extreme Sailing

• Ros Hogbin •

'Above deck the wind gusts to seventy-five miles per hour. The sea spray hits you in the face as if fired from an air rifle and, as you steer the boat, waves knock you off your feet. Huge roller-coaster waves carry on top of them endless rows of short sharp smaller ones, and there is no respite... Down below, condensation drips down the walls and everything is soaking... Grown men, just off watch, have tears rolling down their cheeks as they wait for the blood to start circulating again to their fingertips.'[1]

So wrote Kevin Dufficey, a crew volunteer on the first British Steel Challenge, as he described life racing through the Southern Ocean in 1993.

What is 'extreme sailing'?

The word 'extreme' can be defined as 'the utmost imaginable', which suggests fertile minds pushing at the boundaries of the possible and envisaging things not yet achieved. 'Extreme sailing' can be further defined chronologically. To make any sense, it must be placed in the context of a particular period in yachting history. What was possible in an early period might now seem almost commonplace, but at the time would have been 'the utmost imaginable', given the state of yacht design and the attitude of the yachtsmen of that era. Extreme sailing is by definition a relative term. It describes sailing activity that is ground-breaking for the minds that conceive it and 'close to the edge' for the participants. It takes them beyond what has previously been achieved, to the furthest reaches of human endeavour.

Extreme sailing has always combined competitive challenge, new technology, speed and endurance. It is a modern term with historical resonances. Today, it forms an industry. It attracts sponsors, creates personalities, breaks records and forever looks to the future. But its roots extend back into the mid-1800s, when yacht racing was in its infancy.

Yacht racing – early developments

In order to examine how extreme sailing itself has developed, we must look back at the early years of yacht racing and design. Yacht races such as the America's Cup (1851) were the privileged sport of a few rich owners, with large budgets and boats. The first Transatlantic Race, still the preserve of substantial yachts and wealthy owners, took place in 1866. In 1905 it was won by *Atlantic*, a three-masted schooner, with a record for the best day's run of 341 miles – a record that stood until the second half of the twentieth century. Thus, even at the turn of the last century, competitive speeds were registered and desired by these early sailors.

At the same time, offshore racing for smaller craft was first being considered as a possibility; Thomas Fleming Day set out to demonstrate that a properly designed small yacht, if built and handled well, could go to sea safely. This was a new idea, and the Bermuda Race followed. It had just three competitors and was won by a 38-foot yawl. The competitors were adventurous cruising yachtsmen of the day, who went on to found the Cruising Club of America in 1922.

The British responded by setting up their own race in 1925, the Fastnet. It was of a similar length to the Bermuda Race and organised by the same type of sailors – amateur cruising yachtsmen, who had a keen desire to push their boats in volatile waters and pit their wits against each other. Eight competitors in deep-keeled gaff-rigged boats took part in what was, at the time, a controversial enterprise. The waters around the Fastnet Rock were challenging and the whole concept of ocean racing in a small cruising craft was frowned upon by some. The Royal Cruising Club called it 'unseamanlike' and the Yacht Racing Association, later to become the RYA, said that this type of yacht racing was 'not proper'.

But these adventurous souls, not ones to be held back by such pronouncements, formed the Ocean Racing Club (later the Royal Ocean Racing Club – RORC), which went on to lead the way in the organisation of offshore racing events and handicap regulations. The RORC actively encouraged long distance yacht racing and the building and navigation of sailing vessels in which speed and seaworthiness were combined.

Boat design was at the time undergoing major revision as well. Out went the gaff rig, and in came the Bermudan rig, with increased ease of handling and speed per given sail area, and accompanied by full spinnakers. *Dorade*, a new 52-foot yawl designed in America and dubbed the first 'modern ocean racer', won the 1931 Translatlantic Race in just over 17 days – 66 hours ahead of the rest of the fleet of ten. Mindsets began to shift. Here was conclusive proof that small yachts could be raced safely across the Atlantic. *Dorade* then went on to win the Fastnet that year and again in 1933. This was incentive enough for British yacht designers to produce their own seagoing racing yachts, such as *Maid of Malham* and *Ortac*, which sought to maximise speed in accordance with the handicapping rules of the day, while retaining the robustness of the early cruisers.

The Bermuda and Fastnet races continued – they were fairly short, at under 1,000 miles, but they consistently presented a challenge in terms of endurance. Conditions could change from near calm to gale force headwinds very rapidly, with short, freezing seas to match. A third race, the Sydney to Hobart, which matched the other two in length of course and testing conditions, was set up in 1945. It took place in late December and developed into a major sporting event in the Southern Hemisphere, confronting the often fierce and unpredictable weather in the Tasman Sea and across the Bass Strait.

In the Foreword to Rob Mundle's book *Fatal Storm* Sir James Hardy states, 'It is because ours is a sport which fosters... daring, comradeship, endurance and the risks that the ocean carries with it – that so many of us enjoy offshore sailing.'[2] In other words, it was the challenge of the wind and the waves *per se* that spurred the racers onwards. The oceans were there to be sailed, racing craft were developing fast, and there would always be an element of danger attached to the quest for competitive edge. These three things were enough.

Singlehanded racing – small beginnings

It was not until 1960 that the first singlehanded ocean race took place across the Atlantic from east to west. Blondie Hasler organised and took part in it. His reasons were simple: a) 'to encourage the development of suitable boats, gear and technique for singlehanded ocean work', and b) 'just plain sport'. 'Of course it would have to be a race,' he said, 'because racing is the only branch of yachting in which innovation is accepted... If it were a singlehanded race it would attract plenty of publicity and would encourage a strongly competitive spirit. In order to favour the kind of development I had in mind it would have to be over a long distance with a probability of boisterous sailing conditions.'[3]

Hasler was, however, realistic about the reaction he would receive from the general sailing fraternity: 'Talking to sailing people about it confirmed that most sailing clubs would scream with horror at the idea of my very unorthodox race.' Hasler obtained sponsorship from *The Observer* via its enlightened new sports editor, who recognised in him 'a fellow Corinthian spirit'. The race took place successfully with five competitors, including Hasler, who remained wary about prevalent opinions: 'I know that there are many yachtsmen who are set against the whole idea... I can understand their point of view and I think of them back there waiting to be proved right.'

Jester, *Blondie Hasler's Chinese lug-rigged boat, at the start of the first singlehanded transatlantic race. PHOTO: Bridget Hasler.*

In his book *Blondie*, Ewen Southby-Tailyour summed up the racers' achievements: 'Without their adventurous and courageous spirit this most exacting, exhilarating and pure of sports might have been still-born at the outset, or, at best, been delayed for years until a sceptical press and yachting public... had been more slowly weaned to such contests.'[3] Once again an inventive mind, focused on achieving an untried goal, triumphed, laying the groundwork for future singlehanded racing. The yachting fraternity of the day would have found their imaginations stretched to the limit, as they battled with the very concept of yachtsmen being alone for prolonged periods in small, vulnerable boats, beset by tough sailing conditions and actually seeking to race competitively through them.

Singlehanded circumnavigations

Hasler's work and impetus in galvanising a small group of singlehanders to race competitively across the Atlantic affected Francis Chichester in particular, and it was his thoughts and action that brought about the opening up of the world's oceans and the next phase of round the world sailing. (For a more detailed discussion of the singlehander, see Chapter 7.)

The first chapter of *Gipsy Moth Circles the World* is entitled 'The Dream' and describes in a personal way the thought processes Chichester went through in his quest for his next adventure. He reasoned that it would be possible to circumnavigate the world singlehanded in an 'interesting and attractive' way, including the rounding of Cape Horn, which had been on his mind for years. In common with the majority of racing circumnavigators since then, he identified that this would be the main attraction of the voyage. The very nature of extreme conditions at the Horn lured him. The huge, unfettered Southern Ocean swell combines with very strong wind conditions to produce enormously steep slabs of water which thunder across a suddenly shelving seabed. At the same time, Chichester admitted that the prospect 'terrified' him, while accepting that the Horn had 'a fearsome fascination, and it offered one of the greatest challenges left in the world'.[4]

Chichester's other concern was speed. He wanted to complete the course in the fastest time ever undertaken in a small boat, and thus only allowed himself one stop in Australia. Chichester completed his circumnavigation successfully in 1967, at the age of 66. It was an extraordinary feat and accomplishment which captured the hearts of the nation. Chay Blyth commented on the mood at the time: 'The pattern of events was laid down by Sir Francis Chichester. You're talking the 1960s... we were euphoric, we could do anything – we were rock 'n' roll, flower power... they were euphoric days I can assure you... He had sailed round the world with one stop; there was a great razzamatazz about it.'[5]

In this highly charged 'can do' atmosphere, the time was right for the boundaries of the possible to be pushed back even further. *The Sunday Times* announced their Golden Globe Challenge trophy for the first person to circumnavigate the world non-stop singlehanded. A total of nine competitors set out to achieve this new target, including Chay Blyth and Robin Knox-Johnston, who stated that 'going non-stop round the world was about all there was left to do'.[6] He had his eye on the Frenchmen Tabarly and Moitessier and commented that we would 'never hear the last of it if the French did the non-stop circumnavigation. By rights a Briton should do it first.'[7] Undeterred by his inability to find sponsorship for a new boat, Knox-Johnson entered the race in *Suhaili*, a solid wooden ocean cruiser: 'I didn't have the right boat for the job in so far as racing was concerned. I had absolutely the right boat as far as seaworthiness and my knowledge of the boat was concerned.'[6] With limited speed capabilities, accompanied by the determination to come first, Knox-Johnston left at the beginning of June, aware that he would enter the Southern Ocean early in the season, but willing to take that risk.

The Southern Ocean had become the piece of water at the core of a circumnavigation. 'There's nowhere on earth that you see nature so raw, so powerful. A big wave in the Southern Ocean is awesome... you're just aware of enormous natural power,'[5] Knox-Johnston commented. The development of self steering gear was crucial to his attempt, although it broke beyond repair before he had passed the halfway mark. He spent the rest of the voyage hand-steering, balancing *Suhaili* to sail herself as much as possible and heaving-to in adverse conditions. One by one, the other competitors fell by the wayside. Knox-Johnston was not sure of his final place in the race until Moitessier, who was ahead of him, decided to leave the race and continue on past the Cape of Good Hope again, instead of returning north through the Atlantic. Knox-Johnston completed the course successfully and won the Golden Globe. He had been alone at sea for 313 days, an amazing feat of endurance.

Knox-Johnston's non-stop circumnavigation was a very specific and difficult thing to achieve. To pull it off, it required a certain type of person with commitment, determination and the ability to live at the very edge of the long distance sailing experience. Such people were rare, and naturally Knox-Johnston's success did not open the floodgates for other sailors to follow suit. It did, however, once again bring about a shift in the mindset of what was now deemed possible. Chay Blyth assisted that shift, having been pipped to the post by Knox-Johnston. In his quest for a 'first', he considered a westerly circumnavigation the 'wrong way' round the world, singlehanded and non-stop, stating that this would be 'a voyage to excite any man – and no one had ever attempted it before... possibly the only great sea adventure left at the time'.[8] He persevered with the hunt for sponsorship, and eventually sailed *British Steel*, a 59-foot ketch, to victory in predominantly adverse conditions, knocking 21 days off Knox-Johnston's time in the process.

J R L Anderson, in his Prologue to Blyth's book of the trip, is clear about the man who undertook this 'impossible' voyage and the effect it had on others: 'Most of us, even if we start with wider personal horizons, are compelled to limit them. Chay accepted no such compulsion... [that he was able] to fire other men's imaginations with the peculiar rightness, [and] the necessity of such a task is something quite other.'[8] This comment, succinctly put, might be used to sum up the aspirations of this whole generation of sailors – first-class amateurs, in the classic sense of the word, competing for the love of the sport and not primarily for material gain.

Fully crewed events

Such breakthroughs in singlehanding enabled a new type of venture to be imagined: the fully crewed round the world yacht race. As Knox-Johnston, who was involved in the planning of the first Whitbread, said, 'I think you had to break that barrier of getting round, to make people consider something that no one had really even thought about.'[6] Previously, if they thought about it at all, the sceptics had cited the impossibility of a crew of 12 being able to live and function properly in the narrow confines of a racing boat in such extreme weather conditions and for such long periods of time.

Anthony Churchill and Guy Pearce proposed the first Whitbread Race, which was run by the Royal Naval Sailing Association, and initially partly sponsored by Whitbread. Seventeen yachts took part. Blyth selected a team from the Paratroopers for the event. He reasoned that since they were in the forces a) they would be able to take the year off required to complete the race, b) they had all been trained to withstand mental and physical hardship, and c) they were a known quantity. Blyth drew on his own time with the Paratroopers to train the crew he had picked. 'They [the trainers in the Paratroopers] would push you really hard. The message underneath it all was "you can do it, just take that one step further, the mind will pack up long before the body" – which is true, the mind will always pack up before the body. If the mind can just push you that little bit further, your body will almost certainly go.'[5]

Blyth organised a programme of preparation for them, instigating his own version of a 'team-building' exercise. He took a group of 20 Paratroopers away for a fortnight to an isolated two-bedroom cottage, which approximated life on board a crowded boat – one bathroom, cramped sleeping quarters, no communications and a programme of specific study to be mastered by each man. Before the race, a university psychologist carried out psychometric tests on Blyth and the crew – to his amusement, the results suggested that Blyth did not have a suitable personality for long distance sailing!

In essence, Blyth took a group of fighting men, none of them sailors, and

Chay Blyth churns his way through turbulent oceans on his non-stop single-handed westerly circumnavigation. PHOTO: Chay Blyth.

moulded them into a team that would crew effectively in the Whitbread Race, the length and endurance of which had not been contemplated before as a fully crewed event. Blyth's goal was to take the elapsed time prize in *Great Britain II*, and he achieved his aim. During the race, they faced food and water shortages, three 'man overboards' and the loss of a life: one of three deaths in the 1973 race, reminding everyone concerned of the dangers inherent in extreme sailing. Blyth sums up the attitude of all who took part: 'You don't have to go. You can buy a bag of cotton wool, you can sit inside, but this is a risk sport... doing it, you're taking and accepting the risks that go with it.'[5]

The ethos of the early Whitbreads seems far removed from the professional racing of today. Knox-Johnston took part in the second race in 1977 and commented that he had 'already decided not to take anyone who did not have sailing experience' and that he expected the crew to 'pay their way as far as food was concerned, so as not to lose the feeling of responsibility towards the boat and the race'.[9] In another comment, Knox-Johnston explained how clear it was to him that everyone was treating the second Whitbread as a real race, 'pushing their boats as hard as they could, instead of holding back a little to reduce wear and tear'. In the same chapter, he goes on to say that at one point his crew took out an electric saw while at sea and cut hatches in the coachroof to increase ventilation!

From amateur to professional

Extreme yacht racing in the 1970s, though, was still the preserve of the dedicated and skilled amateur. David Glenn, in his article on design in the January 2000 edition of *Yachting World,* asserts that one of the reasons for the introduction of professionals into the yacht racing scene was to do with changes in design in the 1970s to take advantage of the yacht racing rules of the day. The emphasis moved in the direction of speed, and hence light construction. Human beings themselves became part of this equation, as crews were required to act as 'moveable ballast'. As Glenn says, 'It's not much fun racing an extreme sailing yacht offshore unless you're paid to do it.'[10] Professional status was also conferred and enabled by the development of sponsorship for major campaigns and races, in line with the greater public exposure that the broadcast media provided. Thus the Whitbread (and now Volvo) races moved entirely in the direction of the professional campaign, complete with corporate identity, well-paid skipper and crew, and a requirement to push high-specification boats to their absolute limit.

The quest for speed

As technology advanced, the quest for speed provided an edge of glamour and excitement in the yachting world. By the 1980s, the French had made significant advances in multihull design and construction. The Transatlantic record was fair game; Tabarly took it in 1980 in a little over ten days in his trimaran *Paul Ricard*, and ten years later Serge Madec, on the 75-foot catamaran *Jet Services V,* beat his time down to six and a half days. Weymouth Speed Week, which has hosted a series of record-breaking maximum speed attempts by radical boats, is pushing the current record beyond 45 knots. The world record for a 24-hour run has recently been broken by Grant Dalton's maxi catamaran *Club Med* and currently stands at 625 miles.

The combination of speed and long distance sailing is epitomised by the Jules Verne Trophy, a concept of the 1990s, whereby multihulls must sail non-stop round the world in under 80 days. It was first set up and achieved by Bruno Peyron on *Commodore Explorer* in 1993, who reduced the previous time of 109 days to 79 days. Robin Knox-Johnston and Peter Blake broke that record the following year in *ENZA New Zealand*. Knox-Johnston summed up his thoughts about the challenge at the time: 'You're thinking "Look, I've got this fast boat and I'm pushing her to a sensible limit"... If you can keep her surging at up to 24 knots frequently, you'll probably average 19... Oh it was just fabulous sailing. It was so good, it was just great, a tremendous feeling!'[6]

Great Britain II at the start of the 1973 Whitbread race, crewed by Paratroopers, whom Chay Blyth trained from scratch, instilling in them the mental discipline to compete in this world-class sailing event. PHOTO: *Christopher Waddington.*

And he added: 'Despite eight strong characters living in crowded living conditions, which might be considered a recipe for argument and dissension, we got on pretty well throughout the voyage.'[11]

Full circle back to the amateur

Just when the yacht-racing world had settled down to a future permanently peopled by sponsored professionals, competing in tough trans-ocean and round the world events, Chay Blyth stepped forward in 1989 to announce a different kind of race altogether: the British Steel Challenge. The Challenge was, in essence, an extension of the personal aspirations and achievements of Blyth himself. It offered a match race in identical steel boats to a paying crew – amateurs without previous sailing experience – who would race round the world the wrong way. Not for the first time, in varying degrees, sections of the establishment were sceptical about the scheme. They found it hard to sanction the idea of a collection of novices racing competitively to windward through the most treacherous waters of the world. The crew volunteers, however, applied in droves – 2,000 for 110 available places in the 1992 race, rising to 5,000 entries for the 1996 BT Global Challenge.

In his determination to broaden the extreme sailing experience to include amateurs looking for real adventure and challenge, Blyth has brought the thinking concerning this particular group of sailors full circle: 'What Chay offers in "The World's Toughest Yacht Race" is a real challenge for ordinary people, an adventure of a lifetime and an opportunity to race round the world.'[12] This statement resonates strongly with the adventurous spirit of past achievers. 'They were there... to taste fear, awe and effort as an antidote to the complacency of normal life.'[1]

Chay Blyth has always striven to change attitudes to sailing and alter the 'perception of ocean racing as an elitist sport that can only be done by the professional or the wealthy amateur'.[1] Within his sphere of influence, he has succeeded. His Challenge Business has now grown to encompass a range of events and has recently extended in to America. With each race, training for professional skippers and amateur crews has been developed and refined, in line with professional training standards throughout the sporting world.

Extreme sailing now and tomorrow

Modern sailors participating in a host of events at the edge of 'the possible' rely more and more on training to withstand the physical and mental pressures that go hand in hand with speed and endurance through the world's oceans. Boats such as the Open 60s are increasingly complex. Singlehanded challenges such as the BOC/Around Alone and the Vendée Globe make ever-increasing demands on mind, body and spirit. Radical advances in design for crewed events such as The Race in 2001 prompted Pete Goss to describe his campaign as being 'not a yacht race. It feels more like the early days of the space race as we push back technology to brave an unknown world.'[13]

Extreme sailing begins in the imagination, in those fertile minds pushing at the boundaries of the possible and envisaging things not yet achieved. The oceans of the world have always provided the most testing and enthralling backdrop for these dreams to become reality. Amongst the human race, there will always be an exceptional few who have the minds and skills to take on the wind and waves in a sailing boat; who are not afraid to push themselves to the limit and beyond. The future may not yet have been imagined, but when it is, these extraordinary sailors, filled with a spirit of adventure, will be ready to face and accept the challenges that confront them at the furthest reaches of human endeavour.

REFERENCES

1   *The Challenge*, Chay Blyth and Elaine Thomson, Hodder & Stoughton, London, 1993.
2   *Fatal Storm*, Rob Mundle, Adlard Coles Nautical, London, 1999 and International Marine, Camden, Maine, 2000.
3   *Blondie*, Ewen Southby-Tailyour, Leo Cooper, Yorkshire, 1998.
4   *Gipsy Moth Circles the World*, Francis Chichester, Hodder & Stoughton, London, 1967 and International Marine, Camden, Maine, 2000.
5   Sir Chay Blyth interview, January 2000.
6   Sir Robin Knox-Johnston interview, January 2000.
7   *A World of My Own: The Single-handed Non-stop Circumnavigation of the World in Suhaili*, Robin Knox-Johnston, Cassell, London, 1969 and Morrow, New York, 1970.
8   *The Impossible Voyage*, Chay Blyth, Hodder & Stoughton, London, 1971 and Putnam, New York, 1972.
9   *Last but not Least*, Robin Knox-Johnston, Angus and Robertson, Great Britain, 1978.
10 Design, from 'Milestones in Yachting', *Yachting World*, January 2000.
11 *Beyond Jules Verne*, Robin Knox-Johnston, Hodder & Stoughton, London, 1995.
12 *Global Challenge*, Humphrey Walters, Peter & Rosie Mackie and Andrea Bacon, The Book Guild, Sussex, 1997.
13 www.teamphilips.com website.

Abandon Ship?

• Ros Hogbin •

On rare occasions, severe storms have overwhelmed ocean races. The 1979 Fastnet Race was one of these; the 1998 Sydney to Hobart Race was another. *The Fastnet Inquiry Report* concluded: 'There can be no direct comparison of the results of this race with previous Fastnets as there has been no previous race which has resulted in the loss of more than one life nor have yachts previously been abandoned on anything like the same scale.'[1] John Rousmaniere's *Fastnet Force 10* and Bob Fisher's *The Fastnet Disaster and After* both provide well-researched details of the 1979 storm and its physical effects on participating crews and I have referred to them throughout the chapter. Of the 303 yachts that started the race, only 85 finished; 136 people were rescued from 24 yachts and a total of 15 people died. Of the 24 yachts abandoned, only five were actually lost, believed sunk; the other 19 were recovered.

So what exactly were the conditions that these racers faced? Why did they induce such fear into some, affecting both their ability to cope, and their powers of decision-making? In particular, why did some sailors abandon their yachts to the mercy of the seas and take to their vulnerable liferafts? And are we so sure that we would have acted any differently under the same circumstances?

The physical characteristics of the Fastnet storm

At the height of the storm, the winds registered between force 10 and 11, with some experienced sailors even citing hurricane strength winds above 70 knots. The wind direction was in a state of flux and the initial gale force southerlies, which had built such big seas, veered rapidly to the north-west overnight. The Beaufort scale for force 10 winds (48–55 knots) describes waves as 'very high... with long, overhanging crests, the resulting foam in great patches blown in dense white streaks along the direction of the wind... the tumbling of the sea becomes heavy and shock-like, visibility affected'. The force 11 description mentions 'exceptionally high waves, sea covered with white foam patches, visibility still more reduced'.

These conditions on their own are enough to cause concern, but in the case of the 1979 Fastnet the sharp wind veer caused huge seas to build from more than one direction. One skipper described 'seas coming at one angle with breakers on them, but there were seas coming at another angle also with breakers and then there were the most fearsome things where the two met in the middle'.[2] Several skippers described the waves in this race as the worst they had ever encountered – steeper and more confused even than those experienced in the Southern Ocean and at Cape Horn in round the world races. Chaotic, mountainous cross-seas and multi-directional breaking waves, averaging 50–60 feet in height, caused severe damage to equipment and injury to crew.

The sheer weight of water contained in an average-sized breaker is 10 tons, which may be travelling at speeds in excess of 30 knots. Some of the smaller boats could barely claim to be two-thirds of that weight themselves and were therefore most vulnerable to the storm conditions. Indeed, the damage sustained by the largest yachts in the fleet was almost entirely limited to the failure of some carbon fibre rudders, several of which could not withstand the battering seas. For the smaller boats, the waves were proportionally larger to deal with, and knockdowns were much more likely.

Some 48 per cent of the fleet reported that they had been knocked down to the horizontal and beyond. Some were completely inverted and five yachts maintained positive stability for anything between 30 seconds and five minutes. Most dismastings occurred on yachts that had suffered bad knockdowns, and such damage was consistent with the huge shock loads applied to the rig. Even without a knockdown in storm-force winds one boat commented that 'the mast shook so violently that a running backstay fell off and a spreader cracked'.[2]

The disabling of a yacht due to dismasting is catastrophic, but what happens inside the yacht as a result of a knockdown can be equally demoralising and dangerous. In this race, galley stoves jumped their gimbals, batteries flew out of their boxes, lockers opened and disgorged their tins, inverted companionways provided gaping holes for torrents of seawater, deck seals leaked; and the partially pumped heads on one unfortunate boat regurgitated sewage to soak clothes, bedding and loose equipment down below.

Fastnet racers on the smaller yachts

'The Fastnet is a supreme challenge to ocean racing yachtsmen in British waters... those who go to sea for pleasure must do so in the full knowledge that they may encounter dangers of the highest order.'[3] Every Fastnet participant has always been aware that ocean racing is a risky sport. In some ways, that is precisely the attraction of it – the idea that the wind can be harnessed, that people in a small boat can ride the waves, trim the sails for maximum speed, and compete with others. Many Fastnet racers are amateurs, those who take time off work and put up with the cold and damp because the sailing they do is exhilarating. Their racing is about teamwork, boat performance, acceptable risk, and the simplicity of the natural world.

All skippers prepared themselves and their crews for the 1979 Fastnet Race as best they knew how. Just as the yachts were wide-ranging in size and design, the amateur crews that sailed the smaller boats included seasoned racing veterans as well as near-novices. Skippers made their own judgements as to safety margins, standards of seamanship and navigation, since no qualifications were required by skippers or their crew to enter the race. The burden of responsibility lay with the skipper alone.

For the previous 14 years, the Fastnet had been characterised by light to moderate conditions. Gales were encountered prior to 1963, but the last truly severe storm had taken place in 1957. By 1979, it is possible that the concept of danger had neatly receded from the forefront of the preparing skippers' minds. Anyway, the conditions they were about to face were so far beyond their experience that the impending awfulness would not easily have been imagined.

Although advance forecasting had mentioned the arrival of gale-force winds in the race area, this was at odds with the initial pleasant sailing conditions. The shock came during the night when the predicted gale hit suddenly, increased beyond forecast to force 10, veered sharply, and built tumultuous cross-seas. The work of destruction had begun.

In the midst of the storm

Physical effects on skipper and crew
The smaller yachts rapidly succumbed to the enormity of the violent seas. Different boats used a variety of methods to try to keep a vestige of control. Some used storm sails, some ran off under bare poles with warps streamed to reduce speed, some hove-to, some lay a'hull. Each tactic had its limitations, however, and gave little protection in the face of steep breaking waves – difficult to see in the dark and liable to crash and pound into the smallest yachts at any time.

The knockdowns experienced by nearly half the fleet had a huge effect on the physical state of many racers. Several crew were washed overboard to the extent of their lifelines. Some were rolled back on to their boat as it returned to the upright position; one was left hanging upside-down over the transom; others were dragged by their harnesses through the water. It took ten minutes to haul one skipper on board, even after he had been pulled alongside and his feet dragged up over the toe rail. One boat suffered *five* knockdowns. The crew repeatedly went over the side and were then dumped back into the cockpit, taking more and more of a beating as the knockdowns continued.

A few yachts remained inverted for seconds, and then minutes, and some crew suddenly found themselves underneath the hull, breathing pockets of trapped air. Some managed to dive, unclip their harnesses, and swim free of the wrecked rigging. Even more catastrophic was the loss of life that occurred as a result of harnesses and harness attachment points failing. One yacht rolled slowly through 360°. The crew of this vessel were busy bailing when she was caught by another wave and rolled quickly through 360° again. The three men in the cockpit went overboard and one of them was washed away. One crew member on another boat had a knot in his lifeline. It snapped when a wave threw him overboard, and he disappeared.

Another yacht rolled through 180° and stayed inverted for a number of minutes. A crew member cut the skipper's safety harness to bring him to the surface, but lost his grip on him and the skipper was washed out of reach. A man on another boat that had capsized returned to the cockpit to find his skipper washed away, leaving the clip, safety line and webbing belt of his harness still attached to the yacht. Two men went overboard after a rogue wave hit their yacht. The skipper saw them and headed in their direction as best he could. One, though, had already disappeared beneath the waves and did not surface again. The skipper approached the other survivor and was a few yards from him when a further wave knocked the boat right on top of the man in the water. He did not reappear.

Those who stayed below were not always far from injury themselves. One skipper, who had gone to send a distress call, was hit on the head by a flying tin and slipped in and out of consciousness as a result. One man was left bleeding from a nasty head wound after a knockdown; another split his skull, which quickly resulted in complete exhaustion. Many crews were now existing in survival mode and their plight deepened as they fell prey to seasickness, exhaustion and hypothermia.

Most sailors have suffered from seasickness at one time or another. The violent motion encountered during this particular storm increased susceptibility, rendering the sufferers nauseous, apathetic, anxious and depressed. The crews were also by now exhausted from injuries sustained and the buffetings they were receiving. Their concentration was reduced in the blackness of the night, where everything but the immediate surroundings was invisible to them. They were soaked, and in many cases extremely cold and progressing towards hypothermia.

At a water temperature of 10°C, a human can survive for a maximum of three hours' immersion. At 5°C the time is reduced to one hour. Similarly, core body temperature only needs to fall to 33°C for its automatic temperature regulation mechanism to fail. By the time it has reached 25°C, the person is dead. If the wind-chill factor for soaking bodies is added, sheltered only flimsily from storm-force winds, the risk of incapacity is greatly increased.

Mental effects on skipper and crew

Before the advent of the Fastnet storm, the racing crews would have been in a very positive frame of mind, intent on team effort to maximise boat speed and beat the opposition. Imminent forecasts did not predict anything beyond a gale and, having been lulled into a false sense of security by great sailing and the benign Fastnets of recent years, some crews found the approaching bad weather difficult to accept. Their attitude was wholly one of corporate concentration, to the exclusion of any distraction. Even as the weather began to deteriorate, scenes familiar from past experience or rehearsed in practice manoeuvres would have been put into action, without major detrimental effect.

In his foreword to *Heavy Weather Sailing*, Peter Blake describes what goes through his mind when waiting for rough weather: 'I begin to get a rather hollow feeling in my stomach. Questions spin round in my head. What will the next 24 hours or so bring? Is the yacht properly prepared? Will the forecast (if there is one) be right? Have we enough sea room? Should we have a hot meal now before the seas get up? Is everything properly stowed on deck?'[4] Even sailors with far less experience than Blake would automatically have thought these factors through in their preparation for the race and would have considered themselves equal to whatever nature could throw at them.

But the weather in the 1979 Fastnet really turned nasty, far beyond the expectations of many participants. Life on board the smaller yachts became very uncomfortable and, naturally enough, personal discomfort diverted concentration from the team effort inwards to the unpleasant physical conditions that each crew member now faced. The violent storm created mess, it broke equipment, injured people, and washed fellow crew members away. Stress built to dangerously high levels at this catastrophic turn of events. Mental reserves, at first buoyant, rapidly began to drain away as demoralisation set in.

As the storm developed the initial exhilaration that often comes with an increase in wind and a surge of speed gave way to apprehension, fear and, for many, seasickness. Physical feelings of nausea are always unpleasant, but it is the mental effects that can be far more dangerous. Sickness dominates the affected person's entire existence and distorts their powers of reason and judgement. They only want to lie down quietly and be still; they no longer have any interest in the exertion required for the safety of the boat and crew. Hypothermia also creates mental disturbance. The will to survive recedes and the casualty becomes introverted.

Crews on the boats worst affected by the Fastnet storm were fragmenting. Gone was the sense of purpose that the Fastnet Race normally provided. In its place, morale was at rock-bottom. Crews were beaten up, both mentally and physically, and frightened. Skippers, if not themselves badly injured, were trying to cope with abnormal stress loads, shouldering heavy responsibilities, and attempting to work out survival tactics – when, in some cases, they may have had no direct training in the subject.

With the onset of excessive, even intolerable pressures, 'fight or flight' hormones flood every part of the human body. They increase alertness, but may also be responsible for altering perception and emotional responses to a demanding environment. This can result in confusion, panic, and rash judgements being made.

In the 1979 Fastnet, one such decision was taken when a crew member was washed overboard after a knockdown, and his harness had snapped free of its lifeline. The crew member was spotted, unresponsive, in the water and man-overboard procedures continued with three unsuccessful attempts to pick him up. On the third pass, in difficult conditions, another crew member, who would have been involved in these abortive rescue attempts and undoubtedly hugely frustrated by their failure, suddenly stripped off his foul weather gear and outer clothing and dived in to swim to the unconscious man. This spontaneous reaction to circumstances, given the stormy conditions and high wind-chill factor, proved highly risky and foolhardy. The swimmer failed to reach the man overboard, when a wave washed him out of his way. A further crew member shouted out that the man was dead and the swimmer eventually returned to the safety of the boat. He was by now suffering from hypothermia and shock, forcing the crew to radio a Mayday. He was lifted off the yacht to shore.

Survival and self-preservation dominated the minds of many of these skippers. How best could they extract their crew from the horrifying conditions they had endured for what seemed like an eternity?

Abandon ship?

Fight or flight?

Even for skippers who had talked through a 'what if' worst-case scenario in advance with their crew, the reality of their current situation bore little resemblance to imagined emergencies. Some crew members would have found themselves psychologically stronger than others: 'No matter how much physical equipment the survivor has, his chances of survival are very much weakened if he does not have the right mental equipment with the power to adapt and the will to survive... Men with a minimum of equipment, but with a strong will to live, have survived for long periods, whereas other men with ample equipment have succumbed in less'.[5] 'The positive frame of mind which is necessary to survive the situation becomes *absolutely vital*. It is probably safe to say that more people have lost their lives at sea through having a negative attitude towards survival than have done so through ignorance of what to do with the available survival equipment.'[6] When it came to the crunch, many crews would have had little awareness of just how key their attitude would be in their fight for survival.

In issues concerning the safety of the vessel and her crew, the skipper is the person best able to see the complete picture and make decisions appropriate to the sum of the factors involved. In logical terms, the three main reasons for abandoning ship are:

- when it is on fire;
- when the boat is disabled by failed steering or dismasting and is drifting towards a lee shore;
- when the boat is in imminent danger of sinking.

The *Fastnet Race Inquiry Report* identified a connection between severe knockdowns and the decision to abandon ship. Being washed off the decks of an inverting yacht or being thrown around a somersaulting cabin are undoubtedly horrible experiences. It is easy to see how the cold, rational assessment of such a situation can be affected by confused and panicking crew, injuries, seasickness and companions' loss of life. It is easy to see how the threat of being overwhelmed again, both physically and mentally, or a dismasting and a partially flooded cabin, can cause a skipper or crew to think that the boat is sinking – that the boat *will* sink. Many questions will rush to mind: Just how much water will it take to sink the boat? How sure are we that we can bail out effectively? How long will we be bailing for until help arrives? Is anyone physically capable of bailing now anyway? How long will we have to wait in this crippled boat? What if the wind pushes us into the coast?...

Twenty-four yachts were abandoned. Of these, 17 were 'calculated' desertions, whereby the yacht was only abandoned in conjunction with an expectation that help would arrive shortly. Six yachts were abandoned 'speculatively' and, of those, two actually sank, two had extensive damage to the superstructure and looked as though they would sink, and two yachts remained virtually undamaged. The abandoning of one yacht was 'instinctive'. In other words, the extreme level of discomfort on board overrode a clear assessment of the relevant safety factors – that is, the ability of the boat's hull versus the fabric liferaft to stand up to the storm.

Many crews in the 1979 Fastnet truly believed that their boat was sinking under them. They did not trust their yacht to survive further knockdowns, and they did not think that their boat would remain afloat. On some boats, crew members were nursing bad injuries, were seasick, hypothermic or just plain exhausted. They considered, even if only subconsciously, that the 'fight' was

Yacht Ariadne, *dismasted and abandoned, lying north-west of the Scilly Isles. Her hull survived the storm but four of her crew did not.* PHOTO: *Andrew Besley.*

no longer tenable and that 'flight' was the only option left open to them. Not everyone was able to leave their boat, however. On one, the liferaft refused to inflate. On another boat, surrounded by the debris of a dismasting, the first crew member to be airlifted to a waiting helicopter swam away from the yacht and tried for 20 minutes to secure the rescue harness around his bulky life-jacket. He was eventually lifted clear, hanging on to the cable only by his hands. The rest of the crew thought it wiser to risk staying with the boat.

The skipper of one yacht had been washed away from his boat after a knockdown, and two of the crew showed no signs of life after having been trapped underwater. The other three crew members abandoned ship to the life-raft and were lifted to safety by helicopter an hour later. Meanwhile, the yacht was rolled once again and one of the 'dead' crew members, although injured, recovered consciousness and managed to get back into the cockpit. He winched the second man aboard and resuscitated him, only to watch him die an hour later. He had no liferaft, no flares, and shared the flooded yacht with a corpse. However, he had the will to survive. He set a watch system for himself, found some milk to drink, bailed when he could, and somehow managed to survive for 12 hours until he was rescued by helicopter.

For those Fastnet crews that considered their yachts doomed, taking to the liferaft was the final solution, a decision made only when all other options seemed impossible. They thought that the liferaft would provide safe refuge. For some it did; 14 lives were saved in incidents in which survivors took to liferafts from yachts that were not recovered. For others, the liferafts did not live up to expectations – seven lives were needlessly lost in incidents involving liferafts. The associated yachts were all found afloat after the storm.

But at the time, the perception of what a liferaft could offer to yachtsmen in distress seemed an attractive option. The canopy would provide shelter; the motion would be easier and more comfortable; there were flares on board and emergency rations. Precious few participants had actually spent time surviving in rough weather in a liferaft before this event, but now they were desperate enough to try.

Cut adrift on the open sea

Stepping into a liferaft and cutting the painter free from a foundering yacht is an irreversible act, a last resort. In some respects, those who had abandoned ship had stepped out of the frying pan into the fire. They had left the solid fibreglass hull of their yacht and swapped that environment for a tiny flexible inflatable. Somehow, they expected their survival prospects to improve dramatically. However, their new temporary shelters proved fragile and unpredictable in the midst of the vastness of the turbulent ocean. Without a rigid hull to protect them, they risked exposure. In most cases, conditions were cramped, the motion proved far from comfortable and was liable to induce seasickness in even the hardiest. Most yachts had been abandoned after rescue services had been alerted and the occupants had every hope that they would very shortly be saved. However, their problems were far from over.

The design of some of the liferafts was unequal to the task. Drogues were inefficient and handholds non-existent, their overall stability was questionable, and they were not strong enough to withstand the violence of the waves. One liferaft capsized several times in the space of a few minutes. The drogue was lost and the survivors were caterpaulted into the water. They managed to climb into it again and the same thing happened. This time the structural integrity of the liferaft failed dramatically and the two halves parted. Of the eight men who had abandoned ship, four died, three were washed away, and one drifted out of view on the lower half of the broken liferaft. Another liferaft, with one crew member already on board busily loading stores, parted from the yacht. He drifted helplessly away; the liferaft was overwhelmed and the man died. The rescue services worked extraordinarily

The unconscious owner-skipper of Ariadne *is lifted into the Sea King helicopter. His broken collarbone had prevented him from putting on his lifejacket correctly and he died from a combination of hypothermia and drowning on the way to hospital.* PHOTO: *Andrew Besley.*

hard to pull the stranded Fastnet racers out of the ocean to safety. Where they reached the fragile liferafts in time, they succeeded.

One survivor responded to a criticism about abandoning ship before time by commenting, 'It is worth mentioning the terrific feeling of security once we were in the liferaft, and I'm sure that the psychological boost gained from this enabled us to keep going for a few minutes longer – very valuable moments in my case.'[2] But this was not the case for all crews. In a survival situation, when you are expecting to be rescued, with the rescue vessel in sight, it is very tempting to imagine that you are already home and dry. Many crews had abandoned yachts precisely because they knew that efficient rescuers were nearby. However, it is often in the transfer from liferaft to rescue vessel that mishaps occur. One racing yacht picked up the occupants of a liferaft and the last three survivors were left clinging to the stern of the yacht as the liferaft drifted away from the hull twice. With great difficulty, they were successfully hauled aboard.

One of the saddest cases in the 1979 Fastnet where rescue resulted in fatalities was when a coaster came to the aid of a capsized liferaft. The men clipped on to the upturned raft and several times the coaster tried to position itself for effective rescue in the huge seas. One crew member climbed the pilot ladder successfully; the second reached the ladder, but failed to climb up it and was swept away by a wave. The coaster made two more passes. A further crew member climbed to safety, but the next to try was washed down the side of the coaster and probably sucked into the propeller. The final crewman had forgotten to unclip himself from the liferaft as he attempted to climb the ladder. A wave swept him and the raft away and he drowned.

In the light of experience

Ocean racing is a risky sport and 1979 was an exceptionally bad year for the Fastnet. It is tragic that 15 lives were lost in this one event. Of course, it is possible to make comparisons: boat for boat, almost five times as many boats rolled and twice as many yachts were abandoned in the 1979 Fastnet compared with the 1998 Sydney to Hobart. Hindsight can be sobering and informative, and races carried out under tough conditions often flag a set of safety issues from which we learn and hope to emerge the wiser.

However, the point about an ocean race is that it is there for the racers. The participants have chosen to compete in it and to accept the hand dealt by the weather on that particular occasion. We take part because we want to take part. Whatever conditions we ourselves have experienced and whatever tactics we have employed to sail safely, we will always respect the people who have tried their best to survive when the odds were stacked against them.

REFERENCES

[1] *The Fastnet Race Inquiry Report,* Forbes, Laing, Myatt, to RYA & RORC 1979.
[2] *Fastnet Force 10,* John Rousmaniere, Nautical Books, London, 1980 and Norton, New York, 2000.
[3] *The Fastnet Disaster and After,* Bob Fisher, Pelham Books, London, 1980.
[4] *Heavy Weather Sailing,* Peter Bruce, Thirtieth Anniversary Edition, Adlard Coles Nautical, London, 1999 and International Marine, Camden, Maine, 1999.
[5] *Safety and Survival at Sea,* edited by E C B Lee and Kenneth Lee, Greenhill Books, 1989 and Norton, New York, 1980.
[6] *RORC Manual of Safety and Survival at Sea,* Dag Pike, David & Charles, Newton Abbot, 1993.

FURTHER READING

The Complete Guide to Stress Management, Dr Chandra Patel, Optima, London, 1989 and Plenum, New York, 1991.

Understanding Stress, A Consumer Association publication, Which? Books, edited by Edith Rudinger, 1988.

The Psychology of Sailing: The Sea's Effects on Mind and Body, Michael Stadler, Adlard Coles Nautical, London, 1987 and International Marine, Camden, Maine, 1987.

'Sydney–Hobart 1998 reports', *Yachting World*, March and August 1999.

The Joy of Sailing

• Ros Hogbin •

Why *do* we love to sail so much? What is it that makes us persist beyond the seasickness, the damp and the discomfort that can so often accompany the sport? How is it that sailing can lift the spirit and provide an unforgettable set of experiences for all who participate, from the dinghy sailor to the racer of Open 60s? The challenges of the sailing life have featured strongly in some of the previous chapters, making it easy to forget that there is a positive side to it all. For some, a tentative introduction to life on the water can become compelling – even addictive.

This final chapter looks at some of the different ways in which the mind of the sailor is transformed by joy, using interview material and the written thoughts of the sailors themselves.

The ultimate experience

Ask a group of yachtsmen to define 'the joy of sailing' and many of them come up with one word: 'freedom'. 'Free on the right, free on the left, free everywhere,'[1] as Bernard Moitessier puts it. There is something about the interaction between wind, water and a willing voyager in a small craft that expands the mind and dissolves boundaries. Ellen MacArthur explains: 'I like the freedom, and the fact that you could put a boat on the water anywhere in the world, any piece of sea and go anywhere else in the world... sailing seems so unrestricted.'[2] Out on the ocean, reality beats to a different drum for Robin Knox-Johnston: 'Free of the land, free of society's silly, petty rules. It's real out there. You can't just press a button and change the programme because it gets rough. You've actually got to deal with it, you can't escape it – it's that freedom to run your own life and make your own decisions, with rules that are made by nature, not by man; that's what I like about it.'[3] 'Unconstrained movement in marvellous surroundings,'[4] is how cruising skipper Denise Evans defines her freedom, and Tracy Edwards felt she had

Weighing anchor and waving to friends as we depart from Daniel's Bay on the island of Nuka Hiva in the Marquesas.

achieved it during the 1989 Whitbread: 'I've never been so happy at sea before. I feel totally and utterly free as if the last strings had gone.'[5] For Francis Chichester, freedom was his greatest desire: 'Above all I wanted to be free, as free as a wild sea bird like the stormy petrel, to sail where I liked as long as I liked on the great ocean.'[6]

The great outdoors

In a world where urban concrete covers vast tracts of earth and even the clearest pastoral view may be etched with telegraph poles or smog from a distant chimney stack, the 'lonely sea and the sky' offer the sailor a panorama as yet untainted by human hand. The ability to interact with the natural world and watch creation at its best brings pleasure and meaning to many sailors – such as Pete Goss: 'I love getting out there in the open, in nature. I just feel whole at sea. It's a very wholesome thing. It puts life in perspective.'[7] And Chay Blyth: 'This was a night of oneness with nature, of giving a leg up to the soul. The glories of creation were mine for the looking.'[8] Even after the rigours of his 'impossible voyage', Blyth clung on to what he had discovered at sea: 'Was it all going to be lost, the feeling of well-being that the voyage gave me, of closeness to nature, of why we are really here?'[9]

For Bernard Moitessier, the appearance of marine life enhanced his experience: '25 porpoises... I watch, wonderstruck. More than ten times they repeat the same thing.... I could not tear myself away from all this joy, all this life.'[1] Both Kay Cottee and Pete Goss refer to the fascination of dolphins. Kay Cottee commented: '[A] beautiful school of dolphins swam around the bow for an hour today, [I] could have touched them if I leaned down. Boy, it feels great to be alive out here.'[10] And Pete Goss wrote: 'A streak of light appeared at the bow – a dolphin, its playful path a trail of fluorecent light, was joined by several more and they seemed to compete with each other as they frolicked about the boat. They jumped, individuals, groups, the moon reflecting off their backs. A sense of joy and wellbeing welled up from the bottom of my stomach to catch in my throat. I made a silent promise that one day my children would see a sight like this.'[11]

The sea brings with it a sense of mystery and awe. 'The sound and sight of the sea. It's intoxicating,'[4] comments Denise Evans. 'As for myself,' adds Joshua Slocum in his gentle way, 'the wonderful sea charmed me from the first.'[12] Moitessier attributes musical qualities and life-giving properties to the ocean: 'The entire sea is simply singing in a way I had never known before, and it fills me with what is at once question and answer... The wind, the calms, the fog, the sun are all the same, a single huge presence in which everything mingles and blends into a great light that is life. At times there is anxiety as well. But in the very depths of that anxiety is the inner joy of the sea, and that sweeps everything else away.'[1]

Seascapes are inseparable from skyscapes in their attraction for the sailor. As night follows day, the sun sets in all its magnificence and we can follow its orange-red progress right down to the horizon and stare as it slips quietly below it. 'There was a wonderful sunset soon afterwards,' Knox-Johnston recalls. 'The clouds were all tinted blue... except for one which was golden. A beautiful sight – I wish I could paint.'[13] And Moitessier captures the moment perfectly: 'I watch the sun set and inhale the breath of the open sea. I feel my being blossoming and my joy soars so high that nothing can disturb it.'[1]

After the last of the sun's glow has disappeared and the sky has cooled to its deepest blue, the wonders of the night inspire all passage makers. Chay Blyth provides this vivid description: 'a rippling sea adding a diamanté hem to the star-studded dress which the heavens were wearing'.[8] Both Tracy Edwards and Tony Bullimore have been caught up in the atmosphere. Tracy Edwards says: 'There was a beautiful starry night, tonight, a quarter moon hanging in the sky in front of us, making a silver sea for us to sail on. A huge, huge sky. I lay on deck for hours.'[5] And Tony Bullimore wrote in *Saved*: 'I love night sailing under a clear sky, with the stars reflecting on the water.

With the boat going nicely through the waves, I sit at the helm and glory at the silence and sheer sense of space.'[14]

Day and night, wind and waves, sea and sky – all combine in endless permutations to provide the challenges that the sailor faces. For Chay Blyth, this variation holds his interest: 'The beauty about sailing is that conditions change all the time – one minute you're "in the desert", where there's just rolling, gentle hills with no waves and it'll be a force two and just the swell. And other times of course, you're "in the Lake District" with great hills in front of you.'[15] BT Global Challenge skipper Lin Parker also responds to the changes: 'It's the unpredictability of it... When you actually climb on the deck, you really have no idea whether the next four hours is going to be light winds, sail changes, big waves everywhere... you don't know whether you're going to have a quiet non-eventful watch, where you just point your boat in a straight line for four hours and drink coffee, or whether you're going to be working like mad for four hours, and that's what I really love about it.'[16] For Pete Goss, the intensity of the toughest oceans provide inspiration for him: '[The Southern Ocean] is the most awe-inspiring and invigorating place I have ever been... It is one of the last great wildernesses and being there makes me feel incredibly alive.'[11]

That certain feeling

Pete Goss is not alone in feeling 'alive' when sailing. Moitessier agrees: 'When I go on deck at dawn, I sometimes shout my joy at being alive. I am alive, with all my being. Truly alive.'[1] And Chichester is similarly sensitised by his surroundings: 'All my senses seemed to be sharpened; I perceived and enjoyed the changing character of the sea, the colours of the sky, the slightest change in the noises of the sea and wind; even the differences between light and darkness were strong, and a joy.'[17] Sailing can be an emotional pastime, scattered with moments of heightened awareness and tingling nerve endings. Clare Francis describes highlights from her 1977 Whitbread campaign: 'We were reckless, maybe, but those days were incomparable for a feeling of excitement and achievement... If the surf was a good one, we would hear a great yell of delight from the helmsman, so gripping and exhilarating was the experience.'[18] And Moitessier comments on his happiness: 'I am terrifically happy. I feel so happy, so much at peace with the entire universe, that I am laughing and laughing as I go on deck.'[1]

When some people sail, the competitive element, 'the thrill of the chase', as well as the speed they are able to achieve, gives them immense satisfaction. 'It is difficult to sleep because it is so exciting and gripping trying to get the most speed possible,'[6] Chichester says. Bullimore also attests to such joy: 'I've sailed a racing trimaran... in Canada, doing 28 knots on water like glass with sheer cliffs on each side. It was like being a bullet going down the barrel of a gun. These are rare moments in an incomparable sport.'[14] Likewise, Knox-Johnston commented: 'When you have the confidence, there is nothing like steering a boat at full pelt. The speed is thrilling, reactions have to be fast and that little extra concentration, which leads to gaining an extra yard or two from each wave, brings great rewards.'[19] Mike Golding is stimulated by competitive edge and the intricacies of contemporary racing: 'I enjoy "me versus them"... I used to love tweaking sails, then I'd get into shapes: the shape of the hull, the shape of the rudder. Now it's more strategic, about making good choices in the design but also on the water... The joy for me right now is the complexity of it. I love the depths and how much complexity you have – there's no limit to it. That I find very appealing.'[20]

The boating life and the people factor

Not all sailing takes place in the fast lane. Many cruising skippers gain great satisfaction from the particular boat they own, as well as the sailing they do. 'A wooden sailing vessel is a lovely thing, much more than the sum of her parts,'[21] acknowledges cruising skipper Fran Flutter, and Anne Hammick agrees: 'I enjoy owning and looking after an older boat almost as much as I enjoy sailing her.'[22] Moitessier is captived by the sight of his own boat under sail: 'I gaze at my boat from the top of the mainmast. Her strength, her beauty, her white sails well set on a well found boat.'[1] And Pete Goss describes the relationship between boat and sailor: 'The crew is as good as the boat and the boat is as good as the crew in many ways – you look after it, you care for it, you nurture it – you get out of it what you put into it.'[7] Cruising yachts lend themselves to being pottered on, messed about in, and lived aboard – and even the simplest voyage can bring its pleasures, as cruising skipper Anna Brunyee confirms: 'Going out on a boat you know, preferably your own, with a crew who are keen, a bit of sun, only a slight sea and a good breeze to make the boat respond to the touch of the helm – this would make the sailing complete wherever it is.'[23] Fran Flutter admits: 'I have never found or imagined a more agreeable way of spending time... It is self-contained, unconstrained, with constantly changing locations and impressions, and there are good companions along the way... Physically and mentally I am at home at sea.'[21]

The majority of sailors find great joy in companionship with others, with whom they can share their experiences, as is true for Anne Hammick: 'I find I get on with nearly all the people I meet through sailing – cruising yachties have a much broader outlook than people who've lived all their life in one place.'[22] Chay Blyth refers to his 1973 Whitbread crew in glowing terms: 'The cameraderie is another factor. If you get the catalyst right, which is not always that easy (and it is a challenge to get all of your fellow people "on board", particularly on a long passage), then that is a great thing as well. My crew –

Cruising friends raft up for lunch alongside Huahine in the Society Islands.

we still see each other you know – great guys.'[15] Lin Parker has always considered the training of others as being central to her own fulfilment: 'I love sailing the boat but the actual enjoyment I get – from seeing people who aren't used to sailing suddenly getting the same joy out of sailing – is really good.'[16]

Lasting impressions

Everyone who has put to sea in a small yacht will treasure enduring memories long after they have reached their journey's end. For Pete Goss, it is the splendour of the Southern Ocean, 'its raw, untamed energy gives it a rugged beauty'.[11] For Tania Aebi, it is the simplicity of the sailing life: 'Sailing was special. Thoughts became clearer and simpler at sea, uncluttered by the pressures of responsibilities and familiar habits. It was easy to be happy.'[24] 'The feeling of a new landfall takes some beating,'[23] Anna Brunyee explains, as she expresses a joy common to many passage makers.

During my own circumnavigation the idea of finding an atoll that was so remote and isolated that it could only be reached by boat was something that was fascinating to me. I will never forget arriving at Beveridge Reef, a tiny, submerged coral atoll, hundreds of miles out to sea, between Tonga and the

Cook Islands in the vast South Pacific Ocean. The kidney-shaped reef and the pass into the lagoon were invisible to the naked eye. Our GPS waypoint set at the pass entrance demanded a leap of faith as we edged our way cautiously towards what we hoped was a gap in the jagged coral reef. As we moved ever closer to the waypoint, from out of the vast expanse of sea we finally saw the surf line marking the coral reef, and found the pass. We positioned ourselves centrally and headed for the lagoon. The corally surf roared, yards away on both sides. In a heart-stopping instant, the ocean floor, miles beneath, shallowed to within echo-sounder range and continued up towards us, hovering tantalisingly at 26 feet. At the same time, the inky ocean turned swiftly to aquamarine and turquoise and suddenly we could see the sandy bottom and all manner of marine life in the crystal-clear water. We were through! We anchored a mile away on the far side of the lagoon in soft sand and looked about us. Here we were, balanced atop an invisible coral pinnacle in the middle of the Pacific, and all we could see was water – no sight of land, nothing to spoil the view 360° around the horizon. It was an exquisite experience.

The bigger picture

The grandeur of the oceans encourages an introspection in the marvelling sailor, who is often prompted to ask profound questions, or see something of life's bigger picture. 'Is fate too strong for a man's self-will? Am I so happy because I am doing the sort of thing I was destined for?'[25] asks Chichester. Moitessier adds an element of salvation to his contentment at sea: 'I am continuing non-stop towards the Pacific Islands because I am happy at sea, and perhaps also to save my soul.'[1] For Bullimore, sailing is all-consuming: 'Sailing is more than a hobby or a profession to me – it's a grand passion and a way of life. I can't let go.'[14] And Tracy Edwards poses a question asked from time immemorial – to make sense of the universe she views from the water: 'There has to be a God: how could anything as beautiful as tonight just happen, just be random, with no mind behind it?'[5]

The joy of sailing

However we define it, the joy of sailing exists, amid all the misadventures, crushed expectations and challenges that characterise the more dramatic moments of our time at sea. The people who choose to sail show wisdom in their choice, and are rewarded richly for their efforts. The earth's seascapes, in all their many textures, are without equal – placid, brooding, stormy, mischievous. Sailors have learnt how to harness the elements: to travel and explore, for personal challenge, and competition. Sailing is not just a physical sport; it affects the mind and heart, as well as stretching the limbs. The 'call of the sea' is far-reaching and unquenchable to the many who have at first stepped innocently aboard a sailing yacht.

The mind of the sailor is so many things: inquisitive, at peace, in turmoil, happy, determined and free. Above all, it is open to the unknown and whatever it finds there, within the wind and the waves.

REFERENCES

1   *The Long Way*, Bernard Moitessier, Adlard Coles Nautical, London, 1987 and Sheridan House, Dobbs Ferry, New York, 1995.
2   Ellen MacArthur interview, January 2000.
3   Sir Robin Knox-Johnston interview, January 2000.
4   Lady Denise Evans telephone interview, April 2000.
5   *Maiden*, Tracy Edwards and Tim Madge, Simon & Schuster, London, 1990.
6   *The Romantic Challenge*, Francis Chichester, Cassell, London, 1971 and Coward-McCann & Geoghegan, New York, 1972.
7   Pete Goss interview, February 2000.
8   *Innocent Aboard*, Chay Blyth, Nautical, London, 1970.
9   *The Impossible Voyage*, Chay Blyth, Hodder & Stoughton, London, 1971 and Putnam, New York, 1972.
10 *First Lady – A History-making Solo Voyage Around the World*, Kay Cottee, Pan, Sydney, 1989.
11 *Close to the Wind*, Pete Goss, Headline Book Publishing, London, 1998 and Carroll & Graf, New York, 1999.
12 *Sailing Alone Around the World*, Joshua Slocum, Adlard Coles Nautical, London, 1996 and Penguin, New York, 1999.
13 *A World of My Own: The Single-handed Non-stop Circumnavigation of the World in Suhaili*, Robin Knox-Johnston, Cassell, London, 1969 and Morrow, New York, 1970.
14 *Saved*, Tony Bullimore, Little, Brown & Co, London, 1997.
15 Sir Chay Blyth interview, January 2000.
16 Lin Parker interview, May 2000.
17 *The Lonely Sea and the Sky*, Francis Chichester, Hodder & Stoughton, London, 1964 and Coward-McCann, New York, 1964.
18 *Come Wind or Weather*, Clare Francis, Pelham Books, London, 1978.
19 *Beyond Jules Verne*, Robin Knox-Johnston, Hodder & Stoughton, London, 1995.
20 Mike Golding interview, January 2000.

[21] Fran Flutter written interview, May 2000.

[22] Anne Hammick written interview, May 2000.

[23] Anna Brunyee written interview, May 2000.

[24] *Maiden Voyage*, Tania Aebi, with Bernadette Brennan, Hodder & Stoughton, London, 1989 and Simon & Schuster, New York, 1989.

[25] *Alone Across the Atlantic*, Francis Chichester, Allen & Unwin, London, 1961 and Doubleday, Garden City, New York, 1961.

Book Acknowledgements

The authors would like to thank the following for their permission to include quotations in this book.

Tania Aebi with Bernadette Brennan *Maiden Voyage* Hodder & Stoughton Ltd
Chay Blyth *The Impossible Voyage* Hodder & Stoughton Ltd
Chay Blyth and Elaine Thompson *The Challenge* Hodder & Stoughton Ltd
Tony Bullimore *Saved* Little, Brown & Co
Francis Chichesters *Gipsy Moth Circles the World* Hodder & Stoughton Ltd
    and *Alone Across the Atlantic* Allen & Unwin are reproduced with permis-
    sion of Curtis Brown Group Ltd
Kay Cottee *First Lady – A history-making solo voyage around the world*
    Pan Books
Extracts from Donald Crowhurst's log Hodder & Stoughton Ltd
Tracy Edwards and Tim Madge *Maiden* Simon & Schuster
Clare Francis *Come Hell or High Water* Pelham Books Ltd
Pete Goss *Close to the Wind* Headline Book Publishing Ltd
Naomi James *At One with the Sea* Hutchinson
Robin Knox-Johnston *A World of My Own* Cassell & Co
Nigel Rowe *Around the Big Blue Marble* Aurum Press
Ewen Southby-Tailyour *Blondie* Leo Cooper

Index